# Yor... Mill Town Traditions

## by W.R. Mitchell

with drawings by Ruth Blackburn

Dalesman Books
1978

£1.40

The Dalesman Publishing Company Ltd.,
Clapham (via Lancaster), North Yorkshire

First published 1978

ISBN: 0 85206 483 7

Printed in Great Britain by
Galava Printing Co. Ltd., Hallam Road, Nelson, Lancashire

# Contents

*Cover painting by John Thomlinson. Back cover photographs by courtesy of Keighley Reference Library. Other photographs from the collections of Keighley Library, Graham Hall of Heaton, Bradford, G.J. Mellor and the author.*

*"Residing at new villas in the more salubrious districts were the mill-owners and professional men....."*

# An Introduction

THE NIGHT WATCHMAN for S. Bottomley and Brothers, who had a mill at Buttershaw, or the outskirts of Bradford, carried a muzzle-loading blunderbuss which he discharged at 9 p.m. each day, at the same time shouting: "All's well!" Any woolman who heard his call in the early part of this century would, indeed, believe that all was well. King Wool would reign forever, and his palace was in Bradford!

The West Riding throbbed with industrial vitality. A stranger, his lower jaw drooping with astonishment, saw dramatic millscapes in the valleys and extending up the slopes of the Pennines. Forests of chimneys, discharging black smoke and soot into the misty sky, testified that Yorkshire woollens and worsteds were comfortably meeting a world demand for good cloth. They did this with pride. In 1900, Britain claimed a third of world trade. Of this, one-third of our annual exports consisted of North Country textiles—of Lancashire cotton and Yorkshire wool.

A wool magnate—like John Wesley before him—counted the world as his parish. Fleeces shorn from the backs of sheep that lived under the vast skies of Australia, New Zealand and South Africa, together with wool from the hill sheep of the Dales country, were consigned to Bradford and its neighbours. The drab towns throbbed to the beat of steam-engines driving countless looms; they grated with the movement of iron-shod horses and iron-rimmed wheels on stone setts, as bales of wool were delivered to the hungry mills. The tang of wool grease lay heavily on the humid air. And, in due course, the West Riding despatched its cloth to every country on earth.

"All's well!" cried the watchman with the blunderbuss—a weapon which is preserved in Airedale—and so it would seem to those who had money and influence, if not to the grey mass of the working class. The material achievements were everywhere evident. As Victoria's reign closed, and the new Edwardian period developed, the millscapes continued to spread. Dense concentrations of mills clung to the valley bottoms, where lay main road, railway, canal, river or beck.

Residing at new villas in the more salubrious districts were the mill-owners and professional men, boastful of living rooms that were

5

finely furnished and held thickets of potted palms and ferns; of bedrooms with marble-top washstands, and billiards rooms to which the men could retire after dinner, to smoke cigars and talk wool. At the other social extreme, the poor occupied acres of mean terrace housing, forming the classic grid-iron pattern in the valleys and extending up hill slopes that had gradients where one would have expected nothing more ambitious than drystone walls. The Fosters of Queensbury not only set a huge mill on a hilltop; they erected a 210 ft chimney, which stands today with the visual impact of an exclamation mark. The thrustful Victorian capitalists ignored local topography. In the West Riding, early this century, even the trams went mountaineering.

This book is concerned with West Riding mill town life from 1900 to 1935. As a new century dawned, a woolman in the West Riding would have scoffed if someone had suggested that the textile industry was in decline. Yet the climactic period lay between 1853 and 1873. On the former date, Titus Salt established Saltaire, his range of mill buildings looking like palaces and his model village of 800 homes possessing every advanced facility except a public house. At the end of this golden period, Lister's mill was reared at Manningham, a further assertion of the confidence of private enterprise and West Riding "drive". Afterwards, despite short-lived booms, textiles gradually lost their importance.

Textiles in decline? Nonsense! There had been troubles in the 1890s, when the United States imposed a tariff on imports to that land, and Britain's total export of cloth fell by over two-thirds, but in 1900 trade was picking up strongly again. The woolman at that time would have beamed if he could have foreseen that in 1913 woollen goods to the value of £38m would be exported, or that in the 1914-18 war the mills would busy themselves on large government contracts.

In fact, the war prevented the West Riding from servicing its overseas markets adequately; the boom that followed the war was largely based upon shortages. A wool magnate, like his colleague in cotton, had tended to become complacent; to expect — as in the old days — that customers would storm his offices with orders. The West Riding now had its rivals overseas, for we had exported machines and expertise as well as cloth, and textile industries were being established elsewhere. The rising level of the school-leaving age, and the efforts of the textile unions to improve living standards, robbed the mill-owners of the former large pool of cheap young labour for the machines. In 1910, a half-timer's wage was about 2s.6d. a week!

*Yorkshire Mill Town Traditions* will relate how the folk of the West Riding's textile belt lived, loved, worked, played and died during 35 turbulent, changeful years. The period is historically recent but remote in its spirit and manners from the life of today.

In 1900, the West Riding cherished old ties and loyalties forged by the industrial revolution of many years before. There was a large degree of stability. Everyone knew his place in social life. The 1914-18 denuded the towns of their young men and changed the attitudes of those who survived the carnage in France. In the surge of patriotism, a "Pals" battalion was formed in Bradford, and the town ran that battalion before it was absorbed into the army. Blue uniforms were issued. The "pals" trained in the roller-skating rink and football grounds before being moved into camp at Skipton. Many of the huts were named by their inhabitants, one — "Craig Villa" — being called after the surname of the manager at the Empire Theatre. This pleased him so much that he provided the troops concerned with free cigarettes and passes for the theatre. The battalion moved to Ripon, thence to France, where it was virtually exterminated in a single day on the Somme.

In 1935, when our survey ends, sweeping social changes were under way, diluting the former clannishness and acceptance of the old order. For the working class many new ideas were being absorbed from the radio and cinema which, by the 1930s, held a mass appeal, and the motor car was offering fortunate families a greater mobility.

Slum clearance schemes vastly improved the living conditions, though the rise towards greater affluence was slowed in those areas which, in the late 1920s and early 1930s, suffered from their over-dependence on a single industry during what became known as the Great Depression: a period that still haunts the minds of many old folk in the Riding today. Then a textile town was an unhappy sight, many of its people being crushed by economic forces they could not understand.

This book is concerned mainly with five valleys — Colne, Holme, Calder, Spen, Aire — and has Bradford, Halifax and Huddersfield as its main focal points, yet other communities deserve to be mentioned. They range from small, vigorous towns and villages and hamlets with one or two mills, to factories tucked away from the view of the world in folds between the hills. A lady who wrote to me about her mill memories had been brought up in a mining and farming village betwen Batley and Dewsbury, "and savoured the sweetness and sourness of all three."

In my quest for details of the life that was, I met dozens of people with lively minds and almost total recall of the events of their young days; they were delighted simply to empty their minds of accumulated facts and anecdotes which, collectively, gave me a rich insight into t'owd days and t'owd ways. A Spen Valley woman, recalling a pre-1914 childhood, said: "We didn't have this, and we didn't have t'other. By gum! life were sparse, wasn't it?" An elderly woman living in lush, green Somerset, who returns periodically to Bradford, looked back with deep feeling on a West Riding that was dirty, but distinctive: on incessant talk about combing and carding, tops and noils, mohair and alpaca, woollens and worsteds; of "the fine old Wool Exchange building on Market Street" and "hills fretted with tall mill chimneys."

True individuality was a victim of the heady rush towards better social conditions. It was exemplified by the cloth-capped mill-owner, only a generation or two removed from overlookers and weavers, and by the worker who could be just as proud and forthright as his "maister". The composition of the communities has changed with waves of immigration. In the past, Bradford absorbed Huguenot, Jew, Irish, Russian, German, Lithuanian, Pole and Hungarian. In recent years, the Asians have moved in, and these handsome brown folk now form 9 per cent of the total population.

Familiar buildings in Bradford and elsewhere, have been demolished, to be superseded by office blocks and shops composed of cement and glass. Supermarkets do the work of the few quality shops and countless corner and house-shops at which, in years gone by, you could make purchases and still find the time to chat with the owner about local people and events. It's the gossip for which the old folk of today yearn. The veterans have outlived their friends, but also the age in which they were reared. This book is composed of their memories; it gives them the chance to speak at length about a vanished urban culture.

Cordial thanks are extended to the following who related stories about the mill towns and on whose copious recollections this book is based: K. Armstrong, F. Beardsell, William E. Bennett, Mrs. Blackburn, M. Boocock, Ambrose Broomhead, A. S. Denton, Ian Dewhirst (and the resources of Keighley Reference Library), Mrs. E. Edmondson, R. B. Garrett, Graham Hall (who helped with illustrations), Mrs. Annie Harrison, Mrs. M. F. Harrison, Allan G. Haywood, Tom Hey, John Keavey, J. Milnes, Reg Mitchell, Percy Monkman, E. Oates, Mrs. Doreen Robinson, R. Rowley, Henry Slater, S. L. Snaith, Mrs. G. R. Steel, Maurice G. Stott, Russell Sykes, Mrs. Amy K. Taylor, Mrs. Margaret Wardman, A. M. Warburton.

# Woolmen

WHEN THE EARLY WOOLMEN lifted their eyes to the hills—Pennine hills—they were not seeking a religious experience. From the Pennines came gritstone for building, "soft" water flowing to the expanding towns by way of innumerable "sykes" and "cloughs" and, of course, wool from the hill sheep. They had not far to look for machines, adapting those invented for Lancashire cotton and, in due course, adding some that were distinctly of the West Riding. Among the old, respected families were the Taylors of Batley, Crowthers of Marsden, Amblers of Bradford, Hirsts of the Colne Valley, Crossleys of Halifax, Fosters of Queensbury. A profusion of small-time family firms contributed to what soon became a most extensive and complex textile industry.

The new mill towns sucked in cheap labour, including families from the rural areas of the North and Irish folk displaced from the home acres by potato famine. Housing was provided by the mill-owners or by private enterprise (it was a lucrative period for "jerry-builders") and the towns spread out at random. No one worried unduly about living conditions, for behind the woolmen's success and prosperity was all the grim evidence of a system with growing pains: streets of back-to-back houses, many of which had degenerated into slums, claustrophobic alleyways, primitive sanitation and a generally filthy environment.

By and large, the old mill-owners were not callous men. Many of them had "risen through the ranks". They built their empires at a time when the world had little experience of the effects of industrialisation on people and the environment. It was left to local government to come to grips with the physical and social problems thus created.

Bradford, for all its status as international capital of the wool textile industry, lay in a geographical backwater, its name being derived from a ford over a beck that tumbled from the heights of Thornton. Its worsted mills arose mainly in the new suburbs. Huddersfield, though smaller, produced finer worsteds than did Bradford. In 1900, Huddersfield was almost exclusively a textile town, while nearby Halifax had its mills and also some other important trades. In an old rhyme, Bradford was noted for cash, Halifax for dash and Huddersfield for show.

"Shoddy", based on rags, was the concern of the Heavy Woollen District, of which main centres were Ossett, Dewsbury and Batley. The name "shoddy" is somewhat misleading. Fabrics produced by this means cannot easily be distinguished by layfolk from the best in their class. Within living memory, some three-quarters of the world's shoddy trade passed through Dewsbury.

King Cotton reigned in the Calder Valley, towards Lancashire, especially at Todmorden, which lies in a V-shaped cut in the Pennines, the stem being the main route from Yorkshire, and the forks representing the routes to Rochdale and Burnley. Hebden Bridge manufactured fustian. Brighouse, which alone among the Yorkshire boroughs of old had a red rose on its coat-of-arms, possessed "a bit of everything", including silk, wool and cotton. Keighley, in Airedale, was noted for its textile engineering. So, to a small extent, was Cleckheaton.

Woolmen were not only responsible for the millscapes; they served on local councils, whose grand schemes for public buildings impressed strangers. The design for Bradford's Town Hall (opened in 1873) was based on that of the Palazzio Vecchio in Florence. Wool premises in the area known as Little Germany—a district created through the business flair of immigrants from that land—were cliff-like. Bradford's pride in its men and achievements was arrayed to public view in 1904, when an exhibition was held in the grounds of the newly-opened Cartwright Hall. Huddersfield Town Hall is of Italian style and a substantial tower was erected on Castle Hill to commemorate the 60 bountiful years of Victoria's reign. Halifax Town Hall, a Renaissance style of building, was designed by Sir Charles Barry who, as everyone surely knew, was the architect of the Houses of Parliament.

Few "gaffers" of means could resist the temptation to build a new house away from the mill, at the edge of the town or—in the case of some Bradfordians—at places like Baildon, overswept by moorland breezes. Houses built on a large scale were often ostentatious and in bad taste. A Batley manufacturer was asked by the architect which aspect he wanted and replied: "Gie me one more than t'other chaps have got." At one mill-owner's house, in Airedale, internal woodwork and much of the furniture bear the mark of Robert Thompson, master carver of Kilburn.

Culture of a sort did evolve through possession of money, rather than education and breeding, though the third generation of a mill-owning family could be surprisingly well-educated. A woman who had inherited great wealth from textiles, and lived in a large house, continued the charm, personality and deportment of the mid-Victorian period well into the 20th century. The beds, six feet broad, were fitted with mattresses of swan's down. Meals were taken at a refectory table and an Irish damask table cloth was chosen with care to echo, through its decorations, the main item of food. If this was chicken, then the cloth was embroidered in silk with figures appertaining to chickens. If pheasant was to be served, the selected cloth was adorned with impressions of grouse, partridge and other game birds. Special scissors were used for severing the wings and legs of the cooked fowls.

Early this century, the wool and textile trade centred on Bradford was in the hands of a few "giants of industry", including Sir James Hall, Lister of Manningham — who became the first Lord Masham — Francis Vernon-Willey, E. H. Gates, W. C. (Billy) Gaunt, John Emsley, and others, supported by a considerable number of small-time men and firms. The woolman undoubtedly had character, being "all wood and a yard wide." His word was his bond, and he needed no written orders to cover his transactions. It was said that Billy Gaunt, entering the bank premises which lay under his office, said to the manager: "'Enry, ah want an overdraft." "Yes, Mr. Gaunt, how much?" "Three quarters of a million, 'Enry, and if ah don't get it, ah'll shut b.... bank up." Some woolmen dabbled in anything that offered a return on their money, and both W.C. Gaunt and E.H. Gates financed shows on the London stage. They were capable of great hospitality when in the mood. Billy Gaunt turned his home into a convalescent home for officers during the 1914-18 war. He bought a charabanc to allow the injured men to have day trips.

The High Temple of Wooltopolis was the Wool Exchange, a name abbreviated to 'Change. Some 2,000 woolmen were affiliated. A host of men gathered twice a week at a Victorian structure that soared as though to tickle the passing clouds. You could go on 'Change on any day during the week, and at any desired time, but High 'Change — the period of the main assembly of members — took place from about 2 p.m. until 4 p.m. on Monday and Thursday. Each section of the trade was associated with a specific part of the vast floor of 'Change, its position being found in relation to the marble pillars. 'Change brought together, in one place, the people who could make instant decisions about transactions. An important deal could be negotiated in a trice, culminating with handslaps to seal the bargain. 'Change was also useful for an up-to-date assessment of trading trends.

As an example of this, the management at Merrills, a mill at Morton near Keighley, did a good deal of business with local manufacturers. It seemed to be a tradition of the trade that the spinner in search of business should call upon the manufacturer at his weaving shed. Very seldom did they meet those customers on 'Change. Here, however, personal contact with others in the trade was maintained.

A man who first experienced the mystique of 'Change in 1924 recalls that everyone who attended was correctly dressed. "You never saw anyone without a hat on his head; it was either a felt hat or a billycock. My wife's grandfather, who died in the 1920s, wore a frock coat and a hard hat." Here, in the 1930s, one would be asked the price for 50,000 lb of 2/32s on cheese (2-fold yarn wound on to stiff paper tubes). Management would know this to be for Germany, and that nothing would be heard about the inquiry until prices had been obtained from half-a-dozen competitors. "There is no doubt that large quantities of bunting woven from this 2/32s yarn, for which there was a good demand, went into the manufacture of Hitler's swastika flags. At that time, a farthing per lb. could mean the winning or losing of an order."

Wooltopolis had its many, less formal meeting places. Woolmen entertained important customers at the *Midland* or *Great Northern*. They chatted among themselves at Brown Muffs or Collinson's. The latter restaurant exuded the tantalising smell of roasted coffee on to the pavement, and the owner provided a trio of instrumentalists to play the popular airs of the time. Henry Hardy, who arrived in Bradford from an obscure mid-European town, established a continental-style restaurant at which he conversed with his customers — who came from wool textile centres overseas — in French, German or Spanish.

The bosses were, by and large, shrewd businessmen. They prided themselves on their business acumen, which reduced the natural risks to an acceptable level. They might deal with thousands of pounds on 'Change with little more than a handclasp to seal the bargain. Their most important annual "flutter" concerned the purchase of wool. The season for buying ended in Australia in March, so the mill-owner had then to reckon on the state of the trade in the following August.

One man, who diversified his business interests through a feeling of disillusionment with wool after the 1914-18 war, invested £70,000 in a cement enterprise in Lincolnshire. This astute businessman, who had his wits sharpened by years spent dealing on 'Change, went on to invest £250,000, and in due course he made "a nice profit." Men of commerce were noted for the speed with which they made "brass" and the tenacity of their grip on it once it was secured. There was not only muck in the West Riding: with muck went money!

A tycoon could be ostentatious in the extreme. While lamenting the "crippling" effect of income tax — which, just after the Boer War stood at 11d in the £ — he invested in a country estate. Darley Street in Bradford was nicknamed the Bond Street of Yorkshire because of the evidence of wealth, and it was claimed that every other vehicle to be seen there was a Rolls Royce. Stories were told, and chuckled over, of fortunes made overnight and lost the next day.

Small-time manufacturers in Wooltopolis, who were in the numerical superiority, were by and large austere in their ways. Many were chapelgoers. They were, almost to a man, renown for individual thought and manners, being truly "characters". A topmaker who lived in a village near Bradford, employed his native instinct for "makking brass" by taking surplus eggs from his hens to sell to his workers. One morning, as he waited for a train, an egg rolled from an overful basket and cracked on hitting the platform. He went into the station office to inquire if they had a saucer, with which he could scoop up the egg, muttering: "It'll poach". That topmaker died a millionaire.

Though "tight" in everyday business transactions, the woolmen could be astonishingly generous, with the natural failing of wishing their names to be prominently associated with their deeds. They

created Wooltopolis in a surprisingly short time. The Fielden's, who were King Cotton's main ambassadors in the Calder Valley, gave to Todmorden a Town Hall (opened in 1891), a School of Art and a Unitarian Church. The church itself, costing the family £53,000, dominated not only Fielden Square but half the town. Sir Francis Crossley gave to Halifax its People's Park. The Fosters bestowed on Queensbury a capacious Victoria Hall. What had been a Baptist stronghold swung to the Church of England when Foster "brass" and support were heaped on the parish church. A mill-owner who moved to Eldwick, near Bingley, saw a modest Methodist chapel and remarked: "We'll have a bigger and better place." He quickly added: "I'll pay half the cost."

West Riding fiction presents the mill-owner in an unflattering way. An author's sympathies have invariable been with the workers. There were good and bad manufacturers. The good achieved much for their workers and localities. The distinctive West Riding millscapes were largely their creation. Some became remote from the workers but those who established a small business lived at a house in the mill grounds and began work at the same time as their labour force. They knew their employees to the extent of addressing them daily by their Christian names.

Despite the social differences, there was by and large a chumminess in West Riding life. The boss was known to his workers. At Keighley, throughout the 1930s, three generations of the Smith family, of Dean, Smith and Grace, walked around the town every Saturday morning, following the same route, between the hours of 10 a.m. and noon. The object was to meet any workers who required information or had personal problems. This knowledge of individual workers is reflected in the story of Old Prin (Prince Smith) who, noticing that a worker had just been raised to foreman, ordered that he should be demoted. "Get him back to the bench," he declared. "He's far too good to be a foreman."

There was a fair amount of guile in wool dealings, but generally a man's word was his bond. John Reddihough, who died in 1924, became known as Honest John through his attitude of strict adherence to his given word and his integrity in any financial dealings. So successful was he in business that he was also known as the Wool King of Bradford.

The woolmen cherished their links with the Dales, which lay virtually on the doorstep. Some had homes to the north of the Aire Gap. J. H. Denby, who had strong links with Upper Wharfedale, helped to found an association that fixed the type for Dales-bred sheep. There was a day in 1930 when the Dales came to town. Mr. Denby, with the help of farmer friends, broke the world record for wool "from the sheep's back to finished suit." Americans had accomplished this feat in six hours. Mr. Denby provided overnight accommodation for the farmers. They set up their equipment in the millyard and clipped the wool from the backs of two Lonk ewes and six Swaledales. The fleeces were then taken indoors and the whole process, through to suit-making, took three hours, 20 minutes.

# Mill Days

A COMMON SIGHT IN BRADFORD was that of bales of Australian wool being hoisted to open warehouse doors, where they were expertly caught and dragged inside by the men wearing long, greasy, blue and white-checked "brats" or overalls. Two and three-horse teams heaved and strained while hauling loads of wool up cobbled Godwin Street, with sparks flying from hooves and wheels alike. The teams were later seen slipping and sliding down the hills with empty carts. The wooden brake-blocks, jammed on hard, smouldered under the friction. If an animal fell helpless between the shafts, the carter had the job of untangling horse and harness.

Many of the drays were owned by the railway companies. At the bottom of the steepest hills were "chain horses" attended by lads not long out of school. As a loaded dray approached, the lad hooked the chains attached to the collar of the horse into fitments at the end of the cart shafts, and off they went to the top of the hill. Here the chains were unhooked, the lad would leap on to the horse's back and ride the animal to the bottom of the hill to await another load.

Wool from Antipodes and South Africa was shipped into Hull or Liverpool, and conveyed to Bradford. A good wool-buyer was a man to respect, for a manufacturer, via his agent, bought in five minutes a supply of wool sufficient to last him for 12 months. Business with Australia was undertaken by cable. The messages were in code. A wool-buyer recalls leaving his bed at 4.30 a.m. so as to be at the wool stores by 6 a.m., ready to value the catalogue before the auction began at 3 p.m. Prices were set according to the limits given to him by Bradford or Boston. He once travelled by rail from Melbourne to Perth, living on the train for four days and five nights. Five days were spent valuing at the wool stores. He had orders to buy 15,000 bales. Half an hour before the sale commenced, his orders were cancelled. The market had fallen, and the woolmen of Bradford dare not buy another bale.

In a Bradford warehouse, the bales of wool were never packed tightly together and an ingenious system of checks ensured that wool of a certain quality, from a certain source, could be located in minutes. The warehouse floors became impregnated with grease, and should a fire break out elsewhere in the building a dramatic conflagration was guaranteed. Mill fires were not uncommon. When the night sky held a dull orange glow, the air was filled with the smell of burning grease and wool. Such a fire was so fierce, so uncontrollable, that next morning only a blackened shell remained. In the case of a mill fire, the heavy looms invariably crashed through floor after floor as the building burnt out.

West Riding mills varied enormously in size, if not in general appearance. A mill-owner preferred to put his money into working space and machines rather than squander "brass" on architectural ornamentation. At a typical mill a gateway led into a cobbled yard. Horses were inclined to slide on a smooth surface. The time-office, at the mill gate, was called the "penny oile", from the days when a penny fine was imposed on a late-comer who was then stated to have been "pennied".

The height of a mill chimney was related to the strength of the draught needed by the boiler fire; mill-owners who built high chimneys were not concerned to keep smuts out of the eyes of people living round about. Generally, square chimneys are old, round chimneys being of a later period. Steeplejacks were admired for their bravery, and not a few of them died through a fall. At Yeadon, it was said of a man who was fond of his old clay pipe: "He puffs worse than Billy Murg's chimney."

Steam engine and Lancashire boiler provided the power, and the engine "tenter" was respected by all, from the boss downwards. The engine — which was usually given the name of a woman — had an enormous fly-wheel, and rope drives led to the various floors. A Lancashire boiler, some 30 feet long, with a diameter of eight or nine feet, impressed by its bulk. At one West Riding town a boiler was delivered on a trailer hauled by a traction engine. The metal Titan and its immense load were shortly afterwards reported missing from a parking place outside the mill. When they returned, the traction engine driver explained that he and his mate had fancied some fish and chips. They did not want to walk to the shop!

Barges on the Leeds and Liverpool canal delivered coal. At Morton, "washed smalls" were collected by the firm's own lorry from the canal wharfe. The coal was shovelled on to, and off, the lorry by hand. (The Leeds and Liverpool canal was essentially a Bradford project. The city raised much of the capital, and the company's head office remained in Bradford from the canal's opening until 1850).

Mills were illuminated by gas, and lighting the rows of mantles was an early morning ritual. A weaver who entered before someone had visited it with a taper or matches to light the mantles, found it to be full of fumes. Workers were known to faint from the tang of gas.

Little space was allowed for a mill office. In the days of smalltime manufacturers, the head of a firm might keep all the important documents in his waistcoat pockets. Office furniture was austere: a plain desk, plain chair, and an enamel basin with an enamel jug of water for the boss to wash in after he had been testing "tops". One "office" was simply part of the top sample room. Business meetings were short because those taking part either stood or they leaned against a shelf.

The owner of a mill was usually the manager. Under him, and supervising the efficient running of the departments, were over-lookers, known in some areas as "tuners" for they tuned-up the machines. The equivalent name in the cotton mills was "tackler". In a combing plant, self-owned or on commission, the wool-sorter used his sensitivity of touch and sight as he sorted elements of the fleeces into skeps with regard to length, quality and the amount of fat. A taker-off provided a check on the sorter's operations. Baled wool, harsh and greasy, became delightfully soft and white when scoured. After sorting, and for worsteds, the wool was combed or "carded" into "tops". "Tops" were taken to the drawing room, and their density gradually reduced until the wool was as fine as sewing cotton. There followed the spinning and weaving processes. A woman brought up in Clayton in the 1930s clearly remembers the local bleaching and dyeing mill, a branch of the Bradford Dyers' Association, "where the creamy-coloured bolts of wool on long spindles were shrunk and dyed before being sent to the cloth manufacturers."

Yorkshire looms for worsteds did not chatter as loudly as did looms in the Lancashire cotton sheds; nor were they as densely packed, and the density of the wool absorbed some machine noise. Mill operations were labour-intensive, relying greatly on young people and — though to a lesser extent than in Lancashire — the efforts of women. A form of snobbery existed with regard to the white-collared worker and the mill-hand. The mill worker, and especially a good weaver, was better paid. Shop, office and warehouse staffs tended to be underpaid and grossly overworked.

## The Mill Day Begins

Bells summoned the workers to the early mills. A mill bell in the Haworth area was still being tolled in 1913 — but the buzzer became commonplace. In some areas the knocker-up, usually an old and decrepit man, shuffled round the streets wakening the occupants of certain houses for a charge of a few coppers a week. He rapped on bedroom windows with a long rod topped by wires, or used a long bamboo pole to which some rubber was attached; when the rubber was applied to the window it "produced an awful squeak." Often the clatter of clogs would tell a person freshly woken from sleep who was passing down the street; one learnt to recognise the different treads. Workers left their homes to be at the mill by 6.30 a.m. Women donned wool shawls, large in winter, relatively small in summer, fastening them under the chin with a safety pin. Such shawls could

17

be purchased at Co-ops or draper's shops. Those living near a mill, as at Illingworth, set off for work when they saw the steam rising; it also made a hissing noise. In rural areas, a worker might walk miles to work and, in dark weather, carry a homemade lantern — a carriage candle inside a jam jar, held by wire not string. "The factory hooter or whistle informed you when the engine was starting for the day. If you were unfortunate and late, you would find yourself locked out until breakfast time, that is, 8.30. The halt for breakfast, from 8.30 to 9.00, was called 'being quartered'."

In the first decade of the century, working hours were from 6 a.m. to 6 p.m. during the week and from 6 a.m. to 12.30 p.m. on a Saturday. One woman who left home for work at 5 a.m. recalls that her mother had risen at 4 a.m. to light the fire, boil a kettle and prepare a substantial breakfast. Mother also "put up my jock" which meant that she provided food for the day. Workers who lived far from the mill took their food with them. A meal favoured by a family at Lidget Green was home-made currant teacakes with cheese. It was tied up in a red handkerchief. Currant teacakes in that area were referred to as "Horton Beef". At Yeadon, in the 1920s, the dinner can taken regularly by a small girl to a cousin working at the mill held two basins, one with meat and Yorkshire pudding, the other with rice or sponge pudding. About a dozen boys and girls were on similar missions and "when we came back home, we usually raced each other, but dawdled if the weather was hot."

**The Half-Timers**

Half-time working for children was permitted until 1922. Halifax had 1,057 half-timers in 1917; they were classed as young persons at the age of 13 and were paid about 1s. 6d., rising to 2s. 6d. Two jobs given to youngsters were joining broken threads between thumb and finger (they were dubbed "little pieceners") and taking full bobbins from mules or spinning-frames ("doffers"). A boy starting work half-time was usually proud to be earning money. "You're a real man now." someone observed. The lad replied: "Aye, I'm addling me own brass." Education suffered, but many mill workers later benefited by attending evening classes or meetings of the Workers' Educational Association. A Brighouse woman who would normally have left school in 1906, to work as a half-timer, was granted another two years. A recurrent illness had caused her to miss normal schooling.

A girl aged 12 who began work at Rushforth's in Bingley in 1910 walked to the mill from Gilstead on one half day and, on the other half day she trudged to school at Eldwick. In the following week, the first half of the day was spent at school, and she attended the mill in the afternoon. "We started work at 6 a.m. and had a break at 8 a.m. till 8.30 a.m., then a break for dinner, and we worked every Saturday ... It was very cold, as there was no heating. Everything ran by steam. The overlookers were strict. We had to keep everything spotless. The boss came to look round when we least expected him.

If there was a bit of waste on the floor, we were for it. I was so small, I stood on a box to put the rovings in at the back of the spinning machine. I got the princely sum of 2s. 6d. a week at first, with a few shillings rise as time went on ... We got three day's holiday at Bingley-tide, and two days at Christmas." When she was employed full-time at the age of 14, she received 10s a week. Her family allowed her to keep a shilling a week as spending money.

A Keighley woman who, aged 12, began work at Firth's Mill in 1910 recalls that before a job could be accepted "you had to have enough 'attendances' at school ... We got 4s 8d for the afternoon turn and 5s 4d for the morning turn, plus a 3d bonus on Saturday if you had a full week. At 13 I went full-time and got 10s per week for 55½ hours', plus a bonus of 6d." (At that period, many boys worked for money in the evenings or at weekends, as errand boys, lather boys or attending horses and carts owned by the street traders. Some children hawked firewood).

A woman born in Lidget Green in 1901 recalls that the whole of her family worked "in t'mill". Both her grandfathers and her father were weaving overlookers. Father's two sisters were weavers, and his brother was a jacquard tier-up. They worked from 6 a.m. with a break for breakfast and another for dinner, and — I believe — finished at 5 p.m. They worked on Saturday morning, of course. "Money was scarce. My aunt used to say, now and again, that she was 'pent'. I believe this was in connection with her work. Earnings were related to piece work. When the wages clerk toured the looms on, say, Wednesday or Thursday, he would work out their earnings on the number of pieces of cloth they had woven. If they had done, perhaps, two-thirds of a piece in one loom, he would pay them for it. From then on, until the piece was finished, they were 'pent'."

Bright children who might benefit from a secondary education had to assist an impoverished family by going to the mill. A Keighley boy who left elementary school just after the 1914-18 war had his hopes of a grammar school education dashed when his mother said: "Tha's goin' to no grammar school; tha's goin' into t' mill, and that's that!" He began as a half-timer, and there was a distinct change in the attitude of the teaching staff towards him. A qualified girl spinner taught him the rudiments of spinning.

He was also shown where to get hot water to make tea or cocoa for the other operatives at breakfast time. "Some workers brought tea or cocoa in enamel cans, and warmed the liquid up on the steam pipes. Those with mugs got hot water from the boiler house." A mill-hand at Hipperholme between 1914 and 1917 relates that in the absence of canteen facilities, it was the practise for two boys, usually newcomers, to "brew up", making tea for those who required it. "We had to provide our own pots, and take a 'mashing' of tea or cocoa. Milk was unheard of in this mill. Tea and sugar were screwed up in a piece of newspaper. A big tray was used to carry all the pots, the only source of hot water being the boiler house. Quite often, by the time the boys got back the brew was cold. You ate your snacks where you found it most convenient." A Huddersfield lad of 13 who began work — wage, 5s a week — as a "toilender" on a jerry, a machine that cut the nap from cloth, was under the supervision of an older man. Before the start of each working day, the lad had to visit a pub near the mill for a rum and coffee for his grown-up fellow worker; the cost of this drink was 2d.

A worsted mill at Shipley was the workplace of a 12 year-old when he began as a half-timer on February 23, 1911. His first job, as "bobbin ligger", consisted of carrying a kidney-shaped tub suspended from one shoulder by a leather strap. The tub held empty bobbins for the spinning frame. He was so small he could hardly reach the pegs on a rail where the bobbins had to be placed. Soon he was able to take four bobbins in each hand. When the bobbins on the frames were full, the "doffers" replaced them with empty bobbins. He became a doffer, one of four or five lads who, hearing the head doffer shout "doff 'ere", rushed up to remove the full bobbins. The head doffer re-started the machine as soon as possible.

This lad graduated to being a jobber; he was called upon to oil certain parts of a spinning frame and assist the overlooker to alter the speed of a machine. He also repaired defective driving belts, and kept the centre aisle clear of fluff by wafting it under the machines with an "alley dasher". As a jobber lad, he brewed tea or boiled eggs for workers staying for dinner. The jobber lad also ran errands for pies and cakes. "Friday was the best day, for it meant going out for fish and chips. For every six portions ordered, the shop-keeper would give one portion free. If I had orders for 15 to 20 lots of fish and chips, I had to work out how many to get so that I had money left over, instead of fish and chips."

A woman who started work in Keighley in 1936, at 17s. 10d a week, began at 6.15 a.m. and with breaks for meals a day ended at 5.30 p.m. On Saturdays, the mill was closed at 11.30 a.m. A worker in a silk mill in Bradford, from 1917 to 1930, was paid £1.10s for 54¾ hours. That was before deductions. "There was a bonus scheme though it made little difference over, say, a few months."

## The Daily Grind

Mill life was hard and repetitive. At one mill it took six men to negotiate a constricted flight of steps with a new warp. Accidents were frequent, some of them having amusing consequences. When a belt broke at Bradford mill it slapped an overlooker across his face and threw him to the ground. An anxious worker asked him if he was all right. "Shut up," said the overlooker, "ah'm makkin' enough row for both on us. Damn it — ah'm singing at both ends!"

Workers had a healthy respect for the mill manager, and at a Shipley mill his surname was whispered from frame to frame as he entered the shed. The workers then had time to tidy up their machines before he arrived at their sections. Bad work might be penalised by the imposition of fines. "If a thread broke on a machine, it would cause a lap on the roller. That meant trouble for the spinner or twister. The firm started weghing the laps, and wage deductions were made, the fines being worked out according to the weight of the material."

A feeling of camaradarie existed between overlookers and "hands". It was fostered on the part of the overlookers by a blend of cajolery ("Now you could do better if you tried") and downright blasting sarcasm, if the fault deserved it, just to show the worker who was boss. Some workers did not aspire to be overlookers. An apprentice might be dismissed when his time was served, another apprentice being given his job. It was cheaper than paying full wages.

Overlookers were noted for their drollery rather than lack of wits (as in classic Lancashire tackler tales). When a West Riding over-looker was seen mumbling to himself as he walked down a spinning room, the manager said: "Not so good, talking to yourself, Walter." Replied the overlooker: "Aye, but think on, Ah'm talkin' to a chap wi's a bit o' sense, tha knaws." An overlooker described a new spinner in unflattering terms: "Call yon a spinner? More ends down nor up. Thinks shoo's on a smash and grab raid!" An overlooker could even afford to be sarcastic towards the maister. One, commenting on a batch of yarn going through the spinning room, said: "Ah reckon nowt to it — it's makkin' nowt but dawn", dawn being broken fibres, the lowest-priced worsted spinning waste when sold. A worker was told: "Thou's too slack-set-up to do owt reet."

Conditions in a mill could be intolerable. A woman working at Illingworth in the 1930s recalls "an oily smell from the wool first thing in the morning. The smell seemed to go as the day wor on." A Yeadon woman remembers the terrible sanitation, with only three earth closets for 60 women. All three were infested with rats. "People grumbled, but accepted the conditions. Jobs were so hard to come by." An added hazard in the Heavy Woollen District was provided by fleas. At Batley a man who, in the early 1900s, started up in business with a lean horse and two-wheeled cart, collecting rags in the streets and exchanging them for ruddle stones or "donkey stones", developed a flourishing business. In 10 years he boasted a rag warehouse where he and his son employed Polish immigrants in rag-sorting for the shoddy mills. These Poles, men and women alike, worked long hours for small wages in a dirty job where the population of fleas in the warehouse far outnumbered the employees.

Most boys left the mill after two or three years to take up apprenticeships. Many girls stayed on and continued twisting, winding, weaving or mending, some spending all their working lives at the same mill. Factory lighting was generated by the engine, and at the end of the day, when the engine was stopped, the lights dimmed and went out, "so it was one big rush by the workers to get out before they were in total darkness."

# Life at Home

IT WAS RARELY HOME "SWEET" HOME. The poor, in their mean back-to-back houses, were visited in the 1890s by a representative of the Independent Labour Party, which sprang up in the city largely to secure representation of the people's aspirations through Parliamentary procedure. Most of the working class lived in back-to-backs and the effect was described as one of depressing meanness. Each house had only an upstairs room, a downstairs room and a windowless cellar, with a privy midden to every four or more families.

The grid-iron pattern of terrace housing, laid down in the West Riding during last century, paid scant heed to local topography. Where terraces were set on steep hillsides the foundations were such that the builders could provide a cellar. The infamous back-to-back was part of a row that had been split vertically. In a riverside location, the cellar was so wet it could be used only for the storage of the tin bath. The occupants of the house knew that the river was rising when they heard the clang of the bath lifted from its hook by floodwater! This house was a "one up, one down" and it is recalled that on bath night, one member of the family occupied the bath while the other two found jobs to do outdoors.

No indoor sanitation was possible with the classic back-to-back. If, say, there were 12 houses in a row, then there might be four toilets at the end of the row. Three householders held a key to one toilet. Early this century, earth closets were commonplace; elsewhere the "tippler" toilet was in use. The back-to-back went out of favour in Bradford as early as 1860, when the local authority attempted to prevent further construction (the last to be erected in the district were at Eccleshill in 1898). The government prohibited such housing in 1909, but already many thousands of back-to-backs existed. Not until the large slum clearance schemes of the 1930s did it cease to be a common form of housing in central urban areas.

In the 1880s and 1890s, terrace housing of a more capacious type was being built. The front door opened directly into a living room, but behind were kitchen and scullery. A staircase gave access to two bedrooms above. The rooms were, generally, much larger than with the back-to-back and there might be a backyard, with toilet and midden. Larger terrace houses had passages. A curiosity at Hebden

Bridge, derived from the steep hillsides, was the terrace built in tiers. Two houses stood one above another, the lower house being entered through a door at the front and the upper house by way of a back door at a higher level. A Cleckheaton woman spent her childhood in a single large room, within which was a full suite, two double beds, sink and wringing machine.

In large towns, speculative builders raised new homes by the thousand. Industrialised villages had a nucleus of old weavers' cottages. A family living at Clayton in the 1930s occupied a tiny stone cottage, one in a long row. "Our next door neighbours rented their cottage from us for 7s. 6d per week ... There was no hot water, no electricity, only gaslight in the living room and candles to light the bedrooms. A zinc bath in front of the fire on Friday evenings, filled from the 'copper' of the open range, was the rule, and a draughty outside 'tippler' water-closet was shared by both families. Each cottage in a row had a well of soft, fresh spring-water in the cellar. Stone-flagged floors were the norm."

Cottages owned by a mill at Morton were being rented to workers in the early 1920s for 1s. 6d. to 2s. 6d. a week, a relatively small deduction from a spinner's wage of 32s to 35s a week. Terraces at Keighley, provided by a mill-owner for his workers, became known as the Jewel Box and included streets named Ruby and Emerald. Other evocative street names in Keighley were Mohair and Bengal. Between the wars, many people had lodgers. A Riddlesden woman recalls girls from the mining areas who worked in the mills. "The mill management tried to get them lodgings with respectable people."

Sanitation was crude. At the beginning of this century, Bradford had 22,000 wet ashpits (privy middens) and 9,500 dry ashpits. (Last century, it had been common for householders to toss slops and garbage into the street or into one of Bradford's numerous streams. Dung heaps were scattered throughout the city, and the task of clearing these was given as a punishment to prisoners). At Yeadon, dry rubbish from a household was tossed into a "pothole", a somewhat larger structure than a coalhouse, and having a wooden door. Ashes from the fire were placed in the "ash-hole" between the closets. "We children in Yeadon sang: 'The Corporation dustcart is full up to the brim; the Corporation driver tipped up and tumbled in'. This gruesome thought was enjoyed by the children in my younger days about 1920."

**Indoor Facilities**

A host of West Riding housewives elevated cleanliness to the level of godliness. They rarely stopped working and contrived to turn even the meanest house into a palace. The scrubbing brush and scouring or pumice stone were applied to all external steps and window sills, and even to the flagstones around the house. It was said of one house-proud woman that she polished the nearby tram-lines. Sewing, renovating, repairing and patching clothes, especially the children's, was no less of an accomplishment, and these indomitable women could readily turn to repairing shoes, boots and clogs.

A typical living room-cum-kitchen early this century was dominated visually by a cast iron range. On one side of the fireplace lay a side boiler, with a brass tap, and on the other was an oven. A kitchen table, of deal, was kept white through incessant scrubbing. There might be a chest of drawers or a sideboard, a rocking chair for the elderly and a few mean chairs. Ground floors were commonly stone-flagged; otherwise a householder had a floor of wood covered with linoleum. No house was complete without a multi-coloured "tab" hearth rug, made by members of the family from clothing "cast-offs".

Where a terrace house included a front room, this was used only on infrequent occasions, largely because of the cost of heating. Relatives assembled here when, as "comp'ny", they were entertained to tea on Sunday, or when the parson arrived — which he rarely did — or when a death had occurred. Before funeral parlours were common, the corpse in its coffin lay in state for several days before the funeral. A Cleckheaton woman recalls that her grandparents, whose living space was miniscule, had a "shut-up bed", hinged at one end. It was stored in a vertical position, against a wall, occupying a compartment like a wardrobe. The bedclothes were rolled and stored with the bed.

A roomy cellar-kitchen could be used for three purposes — wash house, bathroom and playroom on wet days. In a corner of one such room was the set-pot, of brick with a lead lining, under which was an efficient little fireplace with an iron door, a sort of miniature furnace. Immediately to the right was an open fireplace, with bars set into the brickwork. To the right of the chimney breast, which served these two fires, was an alcove, and built along it was a waist-high stone slab, extending about six feet. On this the dirty clothes were scrubbed.

The living room fire was needed for heat, cooking and the provision of hot water. At night it was "banked up" with coal slack. The first person to rise in the morning plunged a poker into the black mass and riddled the ashes. Soon a cheerful fire was evident. In terrace housing, coal was kept in the cellar or in a small out-building. If a cellar was used, the fuel was dumped on the pavement to be shovelled through the cellar grate by the householder. It was known for a man to follow a coal cart from the depot and to offer to shovel the coal for 6d, then equivalent to three pints of beer. Poor families bought coal by the bag, paying relatively higher prices than those who bought in bulk. A Bradford firm who supplied small quantities of coal loaned to its customers a small, two-wheeled cart. Children were usually sent to buy coal in this manner so the cart, with its small, cast-iron wheels, was low enough for a small child to be able to get between the shafts.

## Bathing and Clothes-washing

On bath night, the tin bath was brought up from the cellar, or taken from a hook on the outside wall at the back of the house. Placed before the fire, it was filled with hot water from the boiler. Friday evening was usually bath-time, and after the bathing young members of the family might sit before the fire with mugs of cocoa. When a child grew too big he would be given tuppence and told to go to the municipal baths for a slipper bath (the conventional domestic bath). The charge included use of towel and a piece of soap. A woman recalls: "After my bath, I lay in bed at the top of the stairs, listening to the gossip of my parents. The door was left open so that I could see the light, as I was nervous."

The Monday "wash" ritual included possing, scrubbing, boiling, blueing and starching, dampening, folding and ironing clothes. Mother was left limp but happy. Those were the days of scrubbing boards and "dolly tubs". A sunny, breezy day saw acres of clothing on the lines that stretched across every back street. "It took all day," a Yeadon woman relates. "The children had to help. We did so many posses each, and helped to empty wash-tubs and to fold sheets." At another home, mother — "by some clever timing" — arrived at the mangling stage just as her daughter came home from school at five past twelve. "Her voice invariably sang up the cellar steps for me first to put on the 'taters' then to pop downstairs to help. Mind you, this was not the proper ritual 'mangling' but rather the final wringing of the washed and rinsed clothes before they were hung out in the yard; this was my job after our dinner was eaten."

It was important to mangle while the wooden rollers were damp from the morning's wash; dry rollers were useless. It was better, too, if the clothes were slightly damp when brought in from the line. The pile was folded, and divided into several heaps, so that the clothes would not topple over as they were carried down the cellar steps. No clothes basket was large enough to hold it. "The one who turned the handle — my eldest brother, if I could catch him — had to proceed at a sedate pace to give the rollers time to do their pressing job; in theory, the pressure also dispersed the dampness evenly throughout. The really first-rate mangler earned the highest praise as mother — never mum in those days, but sometimes mam — eyed the pile afterwards and said: 'Them won't need a lot of ironing!' "

A type of mangle recalled had the wooden rollers and iron turning wheel. In front was a capacious tub. "A sort of gate was balanced along the top of the tub in two rowlocks; one swung the handle of the gate — we called it a swiller — to and fro to agitate the clothes and the water. It was a much more advanced and refined concept than the old 'dolly' of our grandmother's day. The 'swilling' was by tradition performed to the tune of either *Onward Christian Soldiers* (which, incidentally, was composed in the West Riding) or *John Brown's Body*."

Incidentally, during the early years of this century, iron-moulding was a major industry at Keighley. The products included heavy cast-iron mangles. The two rollers of the mangle were of sycamore. A local man relates: "Iron-moulders believed that their dead comrades were reincarnated as horses. The following story was told. A coal merchant was trying to get his horse to pull a load of coal up a hilly street. Despite whacking and swearing, the horse refused to move. A passer-by observed: "Tha shudna do that." He whispered into one of the horse's ears and the horse moved off briskly. Said the coalman: "What didsta say to t'hoss?" The stranger replied: "Ah said that if tha doesna get up that 'ill, tha'll hev to go back to moulding mangles."

Washing the clothes of richer families earned extra coppers for women who had cheerfully washed the raiment of their own family. In the depressing 1920s, a Cleckheaton woman spent a whole Monday washing and ironing for a family with five sons. She was paid 2s and a "fat pot", which was a 2 lb jar full of dripping from the week-end joint. At that difficult period, with many people jobless and hungry, the dripping was more welcome than the money. A woman remembers Monday wash-day because then "we always had scollops and a slice of treacle and bread for dinner." At another house, "we had cold meat and fried-up potatoes and cabbage".

# Life in the Street

THE STREET WAS AN ENTITY before increasing affluence and greater mobility broke down the tight parochial structure of the mill towns. Every sort of drama was to be observed in the street. No secrets could be kept from the eagle-eyed neighbours. At times, the Street was like one big family. House doors were left wide open all day long; children ran in and out of the houses as they wished, and if an old lady wished to summon help from next door, she would knock on the fireback with a poker. Yet squabbling and bickering between neighbours was not uncommon. At Keighley, I heard of an elderly woman who "got on" with some neighbours but did not speak to others. She tended to boast about the fact that she was "not talking" to a particular woman. Everyone seemed to have a story about the next door neighbour cutting his throat in the yard.

Loneliness was rarely a problem in such a high-density housing area as a street. The women chatted as they washed the windows with their long brushes. Many women put on clean aprons as they waited for their husbands to arrive home with their wages, for the local pub was a temptation on pay day, and it was not unknown for a wife to watch for her husband, ensuring that he did not sneak by the house to the pub and drink his money away.

For children, the Street held mystery and excitement. Spending the Saturday penny at the corner shop was a prolonged ritual. The Street pastimes included playing hop-scotch on the stone flags, skipping under the street gas lamps, whipping "tops" at Easter, running with bowls and hoops, swopping coloured "scraps" for pins or, as a family, attending band concerts in the park and endless picnics on summer days.

A Great Horton man, recalling street life at the dawn of the century, mentions the lamplighter with his ladder and the yeastman who had a lively trade when almost every housewife baked her own bread, probably twice a week when the family was large.

## Street Traders

The fishman with two laden baskets, and men collecting "rags and bones", walked the street and had distinctive cries. The man who sold ice cream in summer returned in winter with roasted chestnuts. "The handbell rung by the ice-cream man on his rounds was the signal for us to run out with our enamel mugs for 'a pennyworth please, mister', and a wafer," it is recalled. Those with half-pennies to spare might buy pots of green or grey peas — "all hot" — from another trader. The knife sharpener (with his machine) was a "hardy annual."

An early visitor to the street was the milkman with horse and float. Milk might be delivered still warm from the cow, the milkman lading it out — plus a few cow hairs — from a kit on the cart. He used a long-handled "dipper". Street cadgers of the period before the 1914-18 war were German bands, four or five young men with instruments. Very occasionally, a man arrived with a dancing bear. Street singers were fairly common. Children greeted the man with tingalaray and monkey. They danced to the music, and fed the monkey, which invariably wore a red jacket. Bedroom windows were closed when the wee creature was on its rounds. Dominic, an Italian living at Keighley, who toured the town with a barrel organ and monkey, also sold ice cream. In the centre of Bradford were regular hawkers of bootlaces who sometimes sold cheap toys. (The Penny Bazaar arrived about 1905).

Early in the century, children played with little danger from traffic, which consisted of the occasional horse-drawn vehicle. It was an unwritten law that no playing outdoors was allowed by parents on Sundays, even if children contrived to miss Sunday School. "You were allowed to go walking but nothing more strenuous until the mid-1930s seemed to bring some relaxation. The local bobby was fairly tolerant, respected, feared even, but inclined to mete out corporal punishment on the spot; he did not rush naughty children to court. No-one seemed to wander far from his own little patch, and we were never bored", it is recalled.

## Games Played By Children

Street games had an endless variety. "Relievo" demanded a tin can, a convenient manhole cover on which to place it and a supply of bolt-holes and hiding places. For football, rolled-up rags served as the ball. An old tennis ball might be used for cricket, heaped stones serving as the wickets. The lad who owned the bat and ball was the self-appointed cricket captain. Those who played hop-scotch were threatened by grown-ups if they planned to chalk on newly-scrubbed flags.

Also remembered are relay races round the houses — "great fun, particularly if your 'opponent' was a girl you were sweet on, in which case you sometimes let her win" — and a game called Labourers, which was described to me thus: "One child was *It*. The others advance towards her chanting: 'Here come five (or six) labourers seeking work'. *It* would say: 'What's your employment?' The others shouted: 'Work'. *It* then said: 'Show it.' The others would mime some occupation on which they had previously agreed — say window-cleaning or painting — and if *It* guessed correctly, she would grab one of the Labourers, who took her place."

The ringing sound of bowls (hoops) being propelled along pavements with iron sticks, known as "shirls", marked out spring's arrival. The girls usually played with wooden hoops. Diabolo became quite a craze. The game consisted of two sticks joined by a cord, and one had to spin and balance on the cord a top-like bobbin. One trick was to spin the bobbin and throw it in the air, catching it again as it descended. Youngsters in the street played "piggy", which consisted of striking a small piece of wood — that had been sharpened at both ends — with a longer striker, usually a piece of broom handle. Your opponent was given a specified number of strides between the start-ring and the final resting place of the piggy. If he managed to reach the piggy, he took over the striking stick.

Games like truth or dare, tin-can squat, hide and seek, leapfrog, and many more, helped to occupy the evenings and holidays. The girls had skipping games, chanting: "Bluebells, cockle-shells, eevory, ivory-over" and "Raspberry, strawberry, gooseberry jam; tell me the name of your young man ..." Taws, as marbles were known, occupied groups of boys.

"Comics" were frequently exchanged: a boy needed only a business capital of one such publication to be in this market regularly. *Magnet, Gem, Funny Wonder, Wizard, Comic Cuts* and *Rover* were popular choices. *The Children's Newspaper* seemed, by common acceptance, too reminiscent of school and compulsive learning for its exchange value on the "market" to be high.

## The Darker Nights

On Mischief Night, children "buzzed" spouts or piled tin cans on doorsteps before knocking on the doors and running away. "We only did it to the people we did not like, or to people who were different. There were quite a lot of odd characters about then." Bonfire Night was celebrated with fireworks, roasted potatoes and "Plot toffee". On Mumming Night "we blackened our faces, and went in little groups to houses and pubs, singing and dancing. Girls usually dressed as boys, either Laurel and Hardy, or Charles Chaplin and Jackie Coogan. Moustaches were made with a burnt cork, dipped in soot."

The steep streets of hill towns were ideally suited to winter sledging. In the memories of old people, winter was colder than it is today. "One could always reckon on all the ponds in the parks being frozen over and fit for skating. Boys who could not afford proper skates bought "dog skates", consisting of pieces of round iron, bent up at each end and sharpened; they were knocked into the soles of the owner's shoes." Adults often pulled old socks over their shoes to enable them to walk more confidently on frozen snow.

No excitement equalled that of the street. There was a general objection when parents shouted for their off-spring, dressed them in good clothes and took on visits to relatives, who might live only a mile away. Visiting grandparents at Oakenshaw, "we children had to go on to a particular flagstone and dance. Before I stood on it, grandfather got a penny and pressed it hard on my head. He pressed it so hard I thought the penny was still there. I had to go and dance the penny off, but it was already in grandfather's pocket! He'd give me two pear-drops from an old cocoa tin that had been used so often it was shiny, like stainless steel."

Mercifully, children were not conscious of poverty. A Keighley man recalls that "we got a slice of jam, or dripping and bread, and away we would go to enjoy ourselves in our own way, exploring the passages and snickets at the town centre. Sometimes we clambered on the roofs as well. I don't recall a single case of wilful damage or vandalism." Keighley children who ventured from the street looked round the Penny Bazaar (later Marks & Spencer's) in Low Street, or went down to Spud Micks for a "warm" at his gleaming brass and cast-iron engine. They dined on hot roast potatoes, with salt from a large box, or a ha'porth of fish bits or chips at Frank Crossleys in Albert Yard, or tripe bits from Gracie's tripe shop on Church Green. Fish and chips, with a choice of "middle" or "tails", cost 2d if they were eaten on the premises. Served on a plate, they were consumed from a wooden shelf against which the customers stood.

A "collective" pursuit from time to time was to gather as many old but clean newspapers as possible and take them round to the local fish and chip shop. "You could always be assured, in return, of a packet of chips suitably garnished with 'crisps' — the residue of the fish batter — to share among a number of hungry young mouths. It was a carefully-conducted manoeuvre. Our hygiene-minded elders kept a watchful eye upon outside toilets if word leaked out. Toilets were usually an excellent source of old newspapers!"

# The Food They Ate

THE SUBJECT OF FOOD has already been broached. The first trickles of saliva will have formed on the reader's chin at the remembrance of old-time meals, for surely food was a major topic. A Yorkshire man declared: "It's thi stomach that 'ods thee back up." We conveniently forget that in straightened times the stable diet for working class folk was bread and jam. Wallaces of Huddersfield proclaimed that they operated "the largest jam factory in Yorkshire."

Baking brought a wholesome smell to every house in the days before packaged foods. Everyone remembers with delight the pleasures of new-baked bread. "My mother baked a stone of flour every week, and from the age of 12 I had to knead it for her. Big crusty loaves, and large flatcake, gave a lovely smell to greet us as we arrived home from school at four o'clock. It was always warm flatcakes and jam for tea on Wednesday."

A Cleckheaton woman recalls that a man arrived in the street with a kit on wheels and he shouted: "Old milk, old milk!" This was "blue" milk — or what was left after cream had been skimmed — and mother used it for baking bread. "She was a great baker, was mother, using her old side oven. She baked plain but wholesome stuff: plain bread, brown teacake and currant teacake, plain teacake and seed teacake. She made lovely sponge cakes, currant loaves and seed loaves."

Bread was a necessity: this had to be home-baked in the proper way. At Huddersfield, the main shopping for one family was carried out on Friday evening. "My job was to carry the flour," recalls a nipper of the period before the 1914-18 war. "For some unknown reason, the flour was always carried in a poke, a sort of cloth bag, and I carried it on my head! I used to love to see the flour come down a chute in the back of the shop and be directed into various bags." The same person remembers that the oatcake man called at the house on Thursday, which was baking day. "How we enjoyed oatcake when it was new and soft. We put treacle on to the cake, then folded it into two and ate it. The remaining oatcake rested on a cord across the fireside and, drying out, was used for soups and stews."

On baking day, the housewife produced fruit loaves and fruit cakes, tea cakes, and flat or "fatty" cakes. The list of favourite recipes is endless. Delicacies included potted meat, suet dumplings, jam roly-poly. "It was more than obvious the Yorkshireman not only liked his food but liked it all home-cooked," recalls a man whose family moved from Cheshire to Bradford. "Capable cook as she was, my mother's culinary expertise expanded greatly with homely guidance and encouragement. It was not all one way entirely. Real Cheshire cheese came more into its own along with such county specialities as 'fritters' with currants or raisins, sponge cake, swiss roll and trifles."

I have mentioned, in a rather disrespectful way, the packaged foods of today. Bought food was cheap and appetising, being readily available at big and small shop outlets alike. It included "savoury ducks", haslett, brawn, potted meat, cow heel, pigs' head or trotters potato with a layer of fish between—once cost 1½d, and a good helping of chips was 1d. A combination of two or three provided many a cheap main meal in those far-off days. They were 'filling' as well as tasty because proper dripping was used for frying." Each town had its pie shops. In Bradford, a steam-pie was the centrepiece of the main window at the *Niagara* in Ivegate or Robert's in Kirkgate. A good helping of pie cost fourpence in the years before 1914. Elsewhere, a plate of green peas could be purchased for a penny. Fourpence would buy you a ham sandwich, made with teacake. It is recalled that so generous was the helping of ham it hung out all round the edges. The coffee taverns sold steak pie, or meat and potato pie, offered with or without gravy. A piece of Yorkshire pudding cost a penny.


## Eating Through the Week

Of home-prepared food, in a working class home, the mid-day meal on Sunday was the week's culinary highspot, and Sunday was memorable if there was "comp'ny for tea" and mother took a tin of fruit from the larder. She might also open a tin of salmon, the fish being prepared in such a way that it was sufficient for six people. The secret lay in mixing the salmon with white bread crumbs, plus a little butter to "bind" it. The family could have easily demolished the Sunday joint of meat at one sitting, but ritualistically part of it was left to be served cold on Monday (wash-day), when mother had quite enough to do without preparing an elaborate hot meal. Wednesday (baking day) introduced some fresh food and replenished the stock of scones, cakes and buns kept in airtight tins in the pantry. The family's meat dish was something like "fry", which was described to me by a Brighouse man as "some monstrous offal-type meal." or it could be "awf a pund o' t'worst end o' t'neck." On Thursday, a family with modest means made do with whatever was going. Friday thoughts turned to fish, and Saturday's lunch, in a mill town, was almost certainly fish and chips bought from a shop. "The routine, if not the food itself, tended to be monotonous." High tea was a strong tradition, being served when the workers returned home shortly after 5.30 p.m.

The close proximity of the countryside had its effect on the diet of many families. Fresh produce could be obtained cheaply at some of the hill farms, or from the allotments. Eggs were available from a farm or from one of the many folk who kept poultry as a sideline. A man who was manager of a mill at Morton relates: "In the late 20s and early 30s, I bought from the overlooker, who kept hens, scores of dozens of eggs at 10d per dozen, and scores of dressed boiling fowls at 2s. 6d each."

Traditional West Riding foods include puddings and pies, parkin and teacakes, treacle tart and cheesecake, scones or Sally Lunns, oven-bottom cake, potted meat, pickles — and jam, lots of jam. Pie and pea suppers were popular at chapel "do's" and ham teas were obligatory at funerals. A housewife could perform wonders with a parcel of meat and bones from the butcher's shop. "My mother put them in a large earthenware stewpot in the fire oven. It gently stewed all afternoon. My father had a large helping when he came home from the mill; he ate the stew with chunks of home-made bread. The coalman called about 8 p.m. for his money and, of course, he had to have a plateful!"

Depending on how the money ran, every family tried to have meat on Sunday dinner-time. A very poor family would have to be satisfied with stewing meat. The chief ambition was to get a joint. "One of the things that happened at the market on a Saturday night was that men floated round the pubs, then back to the market, trying to get a joint at a low price when the butchers were wanting to get rid of the meat before the weekend," a Brighouse man recalls. "The prices of joints fell as the evening wore on. Drunken men were seen clutching pieces of meat as they reeled round the town, going into pubs. By the time the meat arrived at their homes, it was a pretty mangled mess; but it was good meat."

You have not really tasted Yorkshire Pudding unless it was served to you from a roasting tin, being eaten with thick gravy as the first course to a Sunday dinner. The pudding was made with either milk and water, or simply with milk. F. J. Newbolt, who was partial to good beef gravy, wrote "an' when ah sez gravy ah means gravy, not weshin'-ip watter."

A lad who worked for George Hawksby, a Bradford butcher, prior to 1914, carried orders to the more affluent customers on Friday evenings and Saturday mornings. "For this I received half-a-crown a week, and half a pound of sausages, if there were any left. Very often they'd all been sold!" I became an expert at weighing and linking up the sausages, and at cutting off the last vestiges of meat from the bones. These were collected by Waddington's bone waggon, to be rendered down for beef dripping, used by the fish and chip shops. The bits of meat from the bones went into sausages and the

potted meat." George himself made these.

Keeping meat fresh in summer, in the years before electric refrigerators were common, was a nightmare for butchers—hence their desire to sell up the meat on a Saturday evening. The Clear Ice Company, in Bradford, delivered ice in blocks about two feet long and a foot square. The butcher's lad had to break up the ice with hammer and chisel, and he would return to his employer's shop late on Saturday to collect any unsold meat and deliver it to the cold stores run by the Corporation. At Halifax covered market, I heard one trader say: "We've always thought of Bradford as a cow town." He added, with pride: "Halifax is a heifer and bullock town."

I asked a Dewsbury man if West Riding folk had a special fondness for savoury food. He replied: "Aye—if they could afford it!"

## Food in Season

In the West Riding, pre-1914, Christmas feasting was not taken for granted. "Mother might buy a box of dates and various odd luxuries of that sort," says a Brighouse man. Some housewives had a special baking day in October, and aromatic fruit loaves—the famous spicecakes—were put away to ripen for Christmas. For the very poor, Christmas was a mockery. It is related that a mother pawned an old-fashioned sealskin coat to buy a few currants, a small wedge of cheese and other oddments of food, which she baked into small loaves. They were not for the family. "These is for them 'at comes in—understand?" she told her offspring. "Don't dare ask for a bit or I'll skin yer! I'm not havin' you cryin' poverty!" Better-off

35

families tucked in to goose or turkey, with mince pie, followed at tea-time by a gargantuan spread featuring brawn and stand-pies.

Between the world wars, on the hills around Bradford, stood many farms on which turkeys and geese were reared for Christmas sale. One family who purchased a hare at Christmas hung it in the cellar until the new year, by which time it was rather "high". The hare was "jugged" and a bottle or two of Guinness went into the brew. A Bradford woman who specialised in minced meat at Christmas bought a beast's heart, cooked it, and cut it into small pieces, which were placed in a wooden bowl. Her grandson recalls: "We had a chopping knife which exactly fitted the curvature of this bowl. I had to chop, chop, chop away at the meat until my grandmother was satisfied, which she rarely was. She would finish off the job herself!"

Shrovetide Monday was associated with shallow-fried potato scollops. Shrove Tuesday was the day for pancakes. On Ash Wednesday, the main meal was a thick stew with potatoes, known as "hash". Fritters, served on Thursday, were made with a pastry-like dough, mixed with apples, then shaped into round pieces about three inches in diameter and an inch thick. The main course on Friday was fish. In Calderdale, dock pudding has long been made with *Polygonum bistorta,* a plant that thrives locally.

## The Stores

When money was scarce, and supermarkets did not exist, some shops thrived by stocking larger or cheaper provisions than others. John S. Driver, of Girlington, and Abraham Altham, are examples. The latter had a worth-while sideline in selling railway tickets. Competition was intensive in stock-food lines such as butter, which arrived in barrels, the sides of which were knocked out and the butter cut to order with wooden "patters". Tea, lard, bacon and tinned fruit were other food lines to be keenly priced.

The towns had branches of Liptons, Home and Colonial Stores, Maypole Dairy and Meadow Dairy, one or the other being often adjacent to each other. John Rhodes' High Class Grocery, in Darley Street, Bradford, specialised in more exotic and higher-priced provisions. Many mouth-watering delicacies could be seen in the multiplicity of specialist pork butchers' shops spread around the city. They were often of German name and origin. Some of the finest individual pork pies were those bought hot at J. R. Smiths.

The Co-op thrived. That at Bradford, with its many branches, opened a vast emporium with a very pleasant restaurant, in Sunbridge Road, during the mid-1930s. Close by was a Co-operative Hall, available for sub-letting for social activities. There was also the Great Horton Society, the Windhill — serving the northern areas, including Shipley — the Pudsey, the Thornton and others. Halifax Co-op painted its branches in the local bus colours — green and orange.

The Co-op had unswerving support from working folk. A Cleckheaton woman told me: "We were all great Co-opers. I can't think of anything except tea that we bought at another shop. We got the tea from Altham's because they gave a tuppenny ticket with each half pound." With tea in mind, we recall the unique solid-wheeled, solid-tyred red Trojan vans of Brooke Bond's, the tea firm. They were supposedly the only purchaser of such vans, although Trojan was a little known subsidiary of the more famous Leyland Motor Company.

## Corner Shops

The period under review was notable for the thousands of private ventures into retailing. The owners of corner and house shops worked exceptionally long hours, especially on a Saturday. A greengrocer at Bradford visited the wholesale market at 6 a.m. and kept his premises open until midnight. In the Bradford of pre-1914 many small shops closed at 8 p.m. from Monday to Thursday, at from 9 to 10 p.m. on Friday, and at up to midnight on Saturday. A woman with early memories of Manchester Road's many shops remembers that Jaffa oranges were on offer at 10 for 3d and that York Imperial apples, "lovely and crisp", cost a shilling for 3 lb. Market halls provided the convenience of "single stop" shopping long before the supermarkets developed.

The "corner grocer" offered variations on a single food theme to an extent that would bewilder the modern shopper. He graded sugars; they are not all as sweet as each other. He offered crystal sugar, loaf sugar (in the serving of which clippers were needed), cube sugar that was nearly transparent, crystal sugar (small, flat pieces with a glossy appearance), granulated, caster and fine sugars, not to mention the brown sugars, including Jamaica Fines, which were "as dark as the fire-back". A good grocer graded teas to suit the local water supply, and many a small-time grocer would grind his own coffee, using a machine with a big black wheel.

In a child's mind, the corner shop was a wondrous place. Saturday pennies were spent on oranges, liquorice roots, sweets or halfpenny lucky-bags, some of which contained a heart-shaped football card published by Messrs. Bains, who ran a toyshop in North Parade, Bradford. The contents of a lucky-bag were described to me as "a lot of gluey, gooey, stringy stuff that you could chew for ever."

One type of sweet recalled came in small discs, in every possible plastic shade, each disc the size of a coat button, flat on one side, with a curvature on the other side, and each disc was emblazoned with a motto, an example being "I love you." These sweets were gently scented. "We were told never to buy green sweets, from an idea that the cheapest way a manufacturer could get that green colour was by using arsenic. It's possible that this happened, and mothers took no chances and told the children to avoid green." Kali powder was used to make "lemonade" or was sucked from a paper bag through a liquorice tube. Those who took the trouble to shake up liquorice with sugar water in a bottle had a refreshing drink with little outlay.

The corner shop was a focal point for mischief. At one, where the main window was pierced to take the shutter's four bolts, boys pushed soft and sappy pieces of elder through a hole and knocked down the goods. Melting the chocolate by the sun's rays, focussed by magnifying glass, was a trick played in summer. Every shop-keeper was teased by cheeky boys. "Have you any Wild Woodbines? ... Well tame 'em," or "Have you any ice buns? .. Well, skate on 'em."

In the house-shops there might be just a counter or table and some shelves, set up in what would have been the living room of a house. This type of shop helped many a family to eke out father's wage. It remained open on Sundays. "If you went for something and the family was having dinner, one of them would get up and serve you." Another such shop consisted of "a long kitchen table set up under the living room window. The table was covered with boxes of cheap sweets, salt, matches, candles, tapers, sewing needles, pins, Oxo's gravy salt, lemonade and headache powders.

A corner shop specialising in baked food had gas ovens set in the living room of the house. "My mother took over that shop in 1921. She baked teacakes by the hundred. Soon she was making £40 a week, which was very good money then. Of this, a quarter was profit.... A lady came into the shop every Saturday evening; she bought any cakes that were left—perhaps a dozen in all. That lady took the teacakes round to the poor folk of the area."

# Hard Times

BEFORE THE 1914-18 WAR, poverty was accepted as an unfortunate aspect of life. One might see children without shoes or stockings in all weathers. Tramps and vagrants were everywhere in evidence. Many workers were underfed. A Great Horton man remembers the woolcombers, night workers, their faces white, thin and gaunt.

It is with the awesome periods of trade depression in the late 1920s and early 1930s that most memories are concerned. By 1921, over half the textile workers of Huddersfield were idle. Manufacturers went out of business. Mill-workers, on short-time, were stated to be "laiking". The State did little for the downtrodden, and so one small girl trudged each week from Cleckheaton to Roberttown bearing 2s — her family's contribution to the maintenance of the grandparents. "I remember the lethargy of the unemployed. They had plenty of time on their hands, but lacked the energy and spirit to do anything with it," a visitor recalls.

In the General Strike of 1926, the shortage of coal caused many difficulties. "Every house had a coal range which heated the fireside boiler and the oven. Without coal, a family could not even have a pot of tea. Most families I knew at Yeadon could only afford a bag of coal a week, so their stock soon ran out ... Gangs of children set off every morning to walk the two miles to Esholt. I remember the excitement as we took old wood bogeys, pushchairs and old prams across the Engine Fields, down Gill Lane to the railway at Esholt. The trains had stopped running, and we walked along the tracks picking up bits of coal that had fallen from the engines. Men, who went further afield to gather coal, sold sackfuls to the old folk. They also chopped a few trees down in the woods. Once a week we queued at the Trades Union office, and each family received a small wooden box containing about a pound of haddock."

In 1928, a woman who gave birth to a son did not have enough money to cover the modest cost of employing the midwife. When her second son was born in 1930, an aunt arrived with a stuffed beast heart. "The baby died at three months, of bronchitis, but I really hadn't had enough to eat. That wee child hadn't a chance. My aunt lent me £5 to cover the burying." A man existing in Bradford in the late 1920s joined a long queue outside a bakery off Legram's lane, at

6.30 a.m. on a bitterly cold morning. "It was not a queue for bread and cakes. A job was advertised in machine maintenance. It demanded the ability to go round the machine with an oil can. The successful applicant had matriculated at school. He was happy to accept £1. 5s a week."

At Cleckheaton, in the early 1920s, "we'd no work, but I never signed on. I thought: 'It's against my principles to go up to that Labour Exchange and stand in a queue. I'm married. If my husband can't keep me I've no right to get money from the government. I'll have to do something myself'." A Bradford man whose "dole" payments ended after 13 weeks had to face a Mean's Test. "I was visited by one in authority. He asked me what securities and dividends — yes, dividends — I had. Then he caught sight of the piano and said I could sell it. It was my father's piano, and was not for sale. I will not repeat what followed, except to say that the man in authority was glad to get out of the house. I realise that he was only doing his job, but the attitude of him and others was long remembered by a good many 'unfortunates'·of those days."

The workers had little spare cash. "When I went to be a winder, I got 7s 6d per week. My father took it back to the mill-owner, whom he knew, and said: 'Nay, Ben, there isn't enough here to keep thee in cigars for t'week. My lass has worked a whole week for it.' He left the 7s 6d in the office. I got a rise of a shilling a week." A woman reared at Illingworth, near Halifax, says: "We realised at home that our job was to get work and keep it, always hoping things would get better, which they did not."

The effects of depression varied from district to district. Mills with good contracts abroad scarcely lost a month's work. Towns like Brighouse did not close down altogether because there was industrial variety. "If you had 1,500 unemployed out of a labour force of 10,000 it was grim, but not as catastrophic as in towns dependant on one large industry." A Cleckheaton couple, married in 1921, lived comfortably on the husband's four guineas a week he earned as an engineer. "Then the bosses locked out the engineers. The men eventually went back to work. Within three months they had their wage reduced to £2.13s a week. The money was not raised again until the second world war."

A Keighley woman, born in 1920, remembers when her father, an unemployed machine-tool fitter, had a 10s pension for the many wounds he received in the 1914-18 war. "Wednesday — pension day for soldiers — was a special day for me. We generally had fresh cream horns for tea." The father of another Keighley family, and a few others, travelled to Sheffield, looking for work. Mother pawned her wedding ring to pay for his fare and a night's lodgings. and when work was obtained, five or six families went to live around Sheffield. Home-sickness and family ties pulled so strongly that all but one family returned to the home town.

Hungry gipsies, hawkers and beggars were to be seen. Unemployed men played penny whistles or sang for coppers. "They were grateful when my soft-hearted mother offered them a crust of bread and a pot of tea." Keighley had industrial diversity, yet at the height of the depression, about 1931, the vast majority of men were looking for work. The police established a clog fund for needy folk. The mayor's clothing fund was augmented by the proceeds of special events, such as concerts.

It would have been no consolation to an out-of-work man if you had told him that conditions were improving for the majority of people in the country. Social services, child welfare, clinics and maternity care were indeed being improved. A wholesale clearance of slum property, and the re-housing of families in Council houses began when, in many West Riding towns, hearts were still being bruised, if not broken.

# Cradle to the Grave

BRADFORD APPOINTED ITS FIRST municipal midwives in 1917, and the city introduced the country's first scheme for dealing comprehensively with the health of mothers and infants. The first local authority maternity hospital was opened in Bradford. Yet for many thousands of West Riding people little specialist help existed for childbirth until the century was far progressed. The family doctors, and a few dedicated nurses, attended to expectant mothers. At Keighley a doctor called at a house to attend a woman in labour; he found her shovelling coal from the pavement into the cellar. She said: "Go into the house, doctor. I'll have finished shovelling in 10 minutes."

The nurse who was booked for a confinement stayed for a week or 10 days. With no artificial aids to family planning available to the poor, families were generally large. An Oakenshaw woman was the eldest of a family born to a mother who produced her last child when the first was 16 years of age. "My uncle was three months younger than me." At baptism, the former surname of the mother might be used as a Christian name, and Keighley residents included Smith Shackleton, Smith Hanson, Smith Thompson, Bracewell Bowker, Bracewell Smith, Fletcher Foulds. A local butcher, who was baptised Watkinson Wilkinson, had an apprentice named Wilkinson Watkinson.

## Unwillingly to School

The primary schools of pre-1914 are remembered for The Three Rs — four, if you include Religious Instruction — and the harsh discipline, but at one school the poorest children were not caned when it was seen that their hands were chilblained. A few children wore neither footwear nor stockings, and two boys who complained of stomach pains during the afternoon session at a Bradford school, on being questioned by the teacher, said that their dinner had consisted of raw turnip. One of these boys had lost his father in the 1914-18 war. Mother was struggling to raise a family. The father of the other boy was unemployed.

Bradford appointed a school medical officer in 1894, some 13 years before such appointments were compulsory. In 1904-5, the city agitated for powers to feed schoolchildren who were arriving at school in an undernourished state. When Parliament approved the Education (Provision of Meals) Act in 1906, Bradford was the first authority to put that Act into effect. In days of limited personal hygiene, children returned from school with "nits" in their hair. Each evening, mothers used "tooth combs" to locate the "nits", and mother deftly cracked a "nit" with the back of her thumb against the comb or a dinner plate held against the neck.

A man who, when three, had begun school at Greetland was enrolled in the nursery class. A Brighouse man, who also began his education at the age of three, in 1912, says the school he attended took pupils until the age of 14. A fortunate few were able to leave, on scholarship, to continue their studies at a grammar school. St. Andrew's, Brighouse, was a typical primary school, with half-timers still on the books. "The school tended to be pretty boisterous. When some lad who had been in the mill all morning came back to school for the afternoon session, discipline was likely to suffer ... There was no shame about being a half-timer; it was just a fact of life." In Airedale, "we were taught the Three Rs, plus history, geography and singing. Teachers taught only the set curriculum ... I do not remember any tests or examinations." At Cleckheaton, a girl who was good at geography answered teacher's questions long before her class-mates. She was given a penny by the teacher and told to go home.

A typical better-off schoolboy early this century was clothed in a jersey called a "gansey", knickerbocker trousers that buttoned below the knee, long stockings held up by elastic garters worn above the knee, and boots that buttoned, being fastened with the assistance of a special hook. "We wore Eton collars, made from celluloid which could be washed or sponged to keep them clean. Only on Sundays did we have starched linen collars, and these had to go to the laundry to be washed and starched." This lad suffered from pains in his legs. Grandmother jollied him along by saying: "They're only growing pains." The pains were indeed caused by the elastic garters.

The primary teachers mostly spinsters, were dedicated women, good at their job. A teacher gave up working when she was married. "The teachers wore high-necked blouses and long dark skirts. Their long hair was piled up on their heads. If we didn't pay attention, we were caned, or had to stay in school to learn sums, or to write a hundred lines." One headmistress, a strict disciplinarian, was never off-duty. "If we met her in the street we instinctively held our shoulders back, swallowed whatever sweets we were eating, and politely said: 'Good evening, miss.'" By the 1930s, a new kind of teacher was being seen in the Riding. "Young women fresh from college, with new ideas, wore short tweed skirts, beige lisle stockings and brogues. They must have shocked the older teachers with their bobbed hair and modern outlook. Soon all the girls in our class had pigtails."

A man who started at Spring Grove Council School, Huddersfield, under the headship of Godfrey Cooper, recalls that the school was noted for its singing. Madam Clara Butt and her husband Kennerley Rumford were visitors in 1905, and they heard the children sing. It was possible to buy musical instruments through one Cleckheaton school. A girl who purchased a Maidstone violin, price one guinea, paid for it at the rate of one shilling a week. "That's the only time I can ever remember not paying straight down for anything I bought." She became proficient at the violin, was invited to join the school band and helped to play as the children marched into their class-rooms at the start of the sessions.

A woman who spent nine years in Moorside Council School, Ovenden — "years of happiness and interest" — was taught, in addition to the Three Rs, swimming, netball and hockey. The boys were taught football and cricket. She adds: "I'm still amazed at the number of subjects teachers touched on in those brief years." At Cleckheaton, "they taught us how to sew, how to darn ... Very simple sewing but we'd to do it right. You got marks, you know." The child-hood days of a Keighley woman were blighted by Kissing Friday, on which a number of boys waited at the school gates and demanded kisses from the girls. "One boy chased me from Holycroft School to the Damside. What a wasted journey for him. I won hands down!"

A tuck shop near a school at Yeadon is recalled as having three trays on a small counter: the tuppenny, the penny and the ha'penny trays. "We spent ages choosing between Spanish ribbons, gob-stoppers, aniseed balls, lucky bags, sherbert fountains, sugar mice, chocolate nougat (my favourite) or Fry's chocolate cream bars." A grammar school boy discovered that "even if you had the ha'penny for a tram fare home, a better investment was an ounce of broken chocolate from our tuck shop. The old lady concerned was kindly enough to weigh you this out meticulously and sold it normally at four ounces for 2d. It was proper block chocolate, of high standard, but this was the residue of odd bits and pieces which they could not sell at standard price."

During the two years in which her father had no job, a West Riding schoolgirl did not get many pennies, "so I often took to school cone-shaped bags of cocoa and sugar mixed together, or coconut and sugar. We licked our fingers and dipped them into the cocoa..." Children attending school were regularly offered balloons for rags by men who stood outside the gates. At Keighley, tickets were dis-tributed enabling children to attend Russell Street Pictures on Saturday for a halfpenny. "We got an orange or a small stick of rock at the pictures. The cinematograph, hand-operated, frequently broke down. The pianist was often pelted with orange peel."

The State had provided for secondary education for all in 1902. Bright children obtained the few County Minor Scholarships. "If you were of an academic turn of mind, you depended on getting a scholarship and you were drilled before sitting for the examination. If you didn't get a scholarship you just floundered about." Salvation for the unsuccessful lay in attending evening classes, technical institutes and, early in the century, the Mechanics' Institutes. A man who lived in Bradford between 1927 and 1930 recalls attending art school classes for which the tutor was a Mr. Pearson. "Though one sometimes felt tired after a long day's work, attendance at classes — three times a week in my case — did me no harm. In fact I was taught a good deal that has been of value to me in later life."

Bradford Technical College had an enviable standing for its external degrees and professional studies course. Charges were not unreasonable. Everyone paid after the first year of leaving school, and students were attracted from a fairly wide area outside the city, including many other mill towns. There was a loose but close association with the Leeds College of Commerce, with a measure of interchange or exchange of facilities for students requiring really specialised professional training. "Many a milltown lad, myself included, and many lasses, owed a debt of gratitude to one or both of these institutions for excellent help along the road." In 1907, branches of the Workers' Educational Association were formed at Dewsbury and Todmorden, followed by Huddersfield, Halifax and Bradford.

Bradford Grammar School was locally accepted as the top school in the city. "We lesser mortals thought otherwise, and certainly the next tier high schools — we felt — had happier times meeting and mixing, the more especially on the sports fields," says a former high school scholar. "The Grammar Schoolites kept more to their reserved selves." He added that Belle Vue, Grange, Hanson, Carlton and St. Bedes were always old rivals individually, against each other, but were always friendly. Inter-schools football, cricket and swimming matches, with hockey for the girls, were regular and keenly-supported events. The most eagerly awaited of the year, however, was the annual Inter Schools Sports, held on separate afternoons for boys' and for girls' events. Park Avenue cricket ground gave place to Horsfall Playing Fields' fine new sports track at Odsal, when this opened as a major improvement. Attendance was compulsory.

Belle Vue was a foremost participant in sporting events. Additionally, it was bold enough to participate in the Rugby Union football code as well. Under the dynamic leadership of "Peanuts" Bradshaw, a well-respected master and Cambridge Blue, the school could muster a first, second and third rugger teams in addition to formidable football teams. Regular home and away rugger matches were played against Morley Grammar School, Heath School (Halifax), Thornton Grammar School, Prince Henry Grammar School (Otley) and Pannal Ash College (Harrogate), "but never against Bradford Grammar."

45

## In Poor Health

Those were the days of private medicine. Doctors employed debt collectors who visited patients for a few coppers a week. Otherwise the doctors would not have been paid. The earliest recollection of a Cleckheaton woman is when, aged three, she watched the doctor arrive on horseback to attend her father, who had an ailment quite common to iron-moulders — fluid on the knee. A moulder did much kneeling in hot, black sand.

In cases of illness, where there was real poverty, neighbours would lend their best towels, nighties and pillow-cases, so that the invalid could "look nice" for the doctor. The sister of a girl who developed pneumonia recalls that their home was in a street along which passed considerable horse-and-cart traffic. Straw was laid outside the house to deaden the sound of the vehicles, and for the duration of the illness, the Salvation Army discontinued its practice of playing band music in the area. She recovered and is still living — aged 77!

Catching an infectious disease meant a sojourn in an isolation hospital. "The list of diseases was as long as my arm," says a Brighouse man. "Some diseases were killers in the ranks of the under-nourished working class children. If you got infected, they whipped you off to Clifton Hospital. That was the sort of thing you didn't want to happen. It was like going to prison. So you concealed the fact that you had, say, scarlet fever, as best you could."

Dentistry could be crude in the period before 1914. A lad at Huddersfield had toothache one Sunday. The dentist did not work on that day, so mother took him to the doctor, who tried for about five minutes to wrench out the tooth. He was not successful and told mother to bring her son back for further treatment on the following Sunday. "He did not put on anything to numb the pain. I did not go back, of course — and I never complained of toothache again on a Sunday!" Toothache was such a torment, that years ago a chemist might be persuaded to draw a tooth. A Keighley woman who sat in a chair in his shop had the frustration of holding her head back, mouth open, for over two hours. Each time the chemist prepared to extract the tooth, the shop bell rang!

Bill Hall, of Keighley, spent weary months in a large tent in the garden as he recuperated from tuberculosis. A sufferer from pleurisy had hot salt bags pressed on the affected spot. "One night mother woke me up and asked me to fix her a salt bag. I warmed the salt on a shovel over a slow heat and put it in an old sock." Salt long retained the heat, and the same effect was possible using an onion or hot potato poultice or bran.

## Mill-town Courtship

Precocious children were not tolerated by the elders. "Children," they said, "should be seen and not heard!" A Cleckheaton woman said to a neighbour: "By gum, thou's getten two fine lasses." They were, indeed, tipping the scales at 14 stone and 15 stone respectively. The father replied: "Aye, that's wi' snugglin' 'em when they were little, tha knaws."

At courting time, each town and village had its "monkey run", patronised by young people who wanted to "click" with the opposite sex. At Cleckheaton, the "run" was by the Grammar School; at Keighley it was Cavendish Street, and in the small town of Brighouse the four streets at the centre were trodden by young people on Sunday evening, which was the usual evening for courtship. When a young man conversed with a young woman he fancied, it was known as "coppin' on". Some Sunday School Anniversaries were known as "Coppin-on Charities." Courting couples at Keighley were fond of walking over to Steeton, via the Jubilee Tower. They would trudge up Spring Gardens Lane and stop to look at ornamental gates known as the "puzzle gates" from their shape.

In Edwardian times, a young man thinking of romance would dress vividly to impress a girl friend; he would also carry a cane with a silver-knobbed top. There was once a fashion for yellow chamois gloves and spats. A young man who was "going steady" customarily took his girl friend home for tea on Sunday. The picture house later offered double-seats on the back row for courting couples. Going to dances was popular, and quite respectable, in the 1920s and 1930s.

Friends and neighbours showed a lively interest in the activities of courting couples. There were amused glances when a couple was seen. Small children were fond of following the lover and his lass, shouting teasing words. The convention whereby a young man asked his girl's father for permission to marry was usually most embarassing for the father. One, who was approached by his future son-in-law, said: "I have to pop out for five minutes." He fled the house and was not seen again that day!

### Dead and Buried

A West Riding funeral was designed largely to impress the neighbours. Covering the cost was the purpose of many of the old sick clubs that flourished. Friendly societies, such as the Rechabites, warded off the native fear of having to retire to the workhouse, or be buried "on the parish". Every district had a woman known to be good at laying-out the dead. The coffin was set up in the house for a day or two before the funeral, and relatives were invited to view the face of the corpse which involved raising a white handkerchief.

Early this century, John Willie Lancaster, of Bradford, who offered his services as an undertaker, hired his hearse and cabs from Toby Oxley, who had large stables in Annison Street. Toby also owned a large covered yard to house the hearse and some half dozen cabs. Horses for funerals were black, with long black tails, some of which were false! "When John Willie had a funeral the rendezvous with Toby was usually at a public house, where John Willie would buy each of the cab-drivers a gill of ale before the serious business of the day began. The undertaker was clad in long frock coat with black top hat, being tall and thin—the epitome of the lugubrious undertaker."

Funerals were costly. Even the economy class, used by ordinary families, might involve the expenditure of between £20 and £30. "You didn't get much for it by way of show, and it was certainly a lot of money to find when you had a wage of only £2 per week." The neighbours talked about a funeral for days afterwards. The coffin must be of the best English oak. One would commonly hear that "they put 'im away wi' ham an' tongue."

As the cortege left the house, the blinds and curtains in neighbouring houses were drawn "out of respect". No excessive noise was tolerated. Later, back at the home of the deceased, there would be a solemn, often tense, sharing-out of furniture and bed-linen among relatives.

# Speech and Song

WAS THERE A DISTINCTIVE BREED that might be termed "West Riding"? Perhaps, though quite apart from the native Pennine population there were the immigrant communities, attracted by work in the mills. An overwhelming Yorkshire character was once detectable. A person who expressed it was sturdy, fiercely loyal to the home patch, proud and independent "not beholden to onnybody", with an innate self-respect that was revealed in giving a good day's labour. One detects a disdain of the shiftless or lazy fellows, who were described as "offald". Big Town Folk could be grey, colourless, forever complaining—though a dour manner often masked a sense of fun. West Riding fun was blunt, direct, even rude; it was totally lacking in finesse. Taciturnity, another old-time characteristic, has been summed up as "the ability to say nowt in a long time." John Hartley, the Yorkshire dialect poet, had declared: "If a chap knaws nowt but says nowt, fowk'll oft think he knaws summat!"

The West Riding type had no time for the sham. "Tha talks an' says nowt," a man might say to a blatherer. Words in common used tended to be hard, forceful, such as tew (from tow) for struggle, thoil (cannot bear), agate (to be pre-occupied with work). A confused

A STUDY OF BRADFORD IN THE LATE 19th CENTURY, SHOWING
THE WOOL EXCHANGE

A feature of the old Halifax Zoo.

# Less Serious Moods

Members of the Greeasy Chin Club at Sowerby Bridge in 1932.

One of the last horse-drawn trams at Keighley.

# Farewell to the Horse

An early mail van, photographed at Huddersfield.

Inside a working class home at Keighley.

# Life in the Street

Morning milk delivery by horse and cart at Keighley.

Manningham Lane, at the junction of Bowland Street. Note the superb gas-lamp.

# On the Main Road

Briggate, Shipley, looking towards Saltaire, about 1906.

South-west view of the mills at Saltaire.

# Large-Scale Manufacturing

The vast mill of Lister and Company at Manningham, Bradford

Mill, rail, river — an aerial view of the Colne Valley.

# Mill Town Vistas

Small town, a quite recent study at Brighouse

The first of Bradford's trackless cars, pictured in 1911.

# A Welcome to the New

An early lorry used by a textile firm, this being Unwin Freres of Bradford, pictured in the early 1920s.

man is "moithered". There is a laziness in the speech of some areas. A visitor thought she was listening to a Chinese when she heard: "Whowoshewi?" (Who was she with).

Where maister and worker often lived close to each other, they may, indeed, have attended the same school — and thus there was little cap-doffing to those with money. The pompous and authoritarian were quietly ridiculed, as over the motto of Brighouse — "By Labour and Prudence." Prudence, it was claimed, was a typist at the Town Hall in 1893! Overall, there was a realistic attitude to life. A man living near Halifax, after telling me of his hard life, said: "I've had to work hard for many years, and there's nowt at the end of it."

A thin vein of sentimentality ran through the West Riding character, to be nurtured by music hall comics and expressed by the old dialect poets, such as John Hartley, who died in 1915. An engine-man at a mill by the Spen came close to expressing warm feelings towards a weaver when he nicknamed her Flywheel — "because tha's quick, like that flywheel 'at's goin' rahnd." A grim vein of humour is expressed in a hundred classic funeral stories. The feeling is not one of morbidity. Life was cheap in the old days; people became reconciled to death.

The Yorkshire anthem, *On Ilkla' Moor Baht 'At,* links courtship with death! It was composed during the day-trip of a Halifax church choir to Ilkley Moor. A man and the girl he fancied left the party for a while. On their return, the man was asked: "Wheear 'as ta bin' sin' Ah saw thee?" He'd been a-courtin' Mary-Jane — baht 'at, or without a hat, which meant that he ran the risk of catching cold, and dying. Incidentally, the song, spontaneously composed, was sung to a hymn tune called *Cranbrook.* Returning to the word "baht", for without, it is related at Saltaire that visitors of years ago who saw a newly-painted dray on which were the words "Sir Titus Salt, Bart, Sons and Company Limited," were told: "Well, even Sir Titus 'ed 'is ups an' dahns i' life. He wor baht sons an' 'is company wor limited." To appreciate a true West Riding ballad, listen to the Holmfirth anthem, *Pratty Flowers.*

Your West Riding man has the reputation of being hard-headed, unemotional and forthright and these qualities characterised the owner of a row of back-to-backs at Littletown who arrived at the premises every Saturday to collect the rent. He said to one housewife: "Sitha, come 'ere." He showed her the house next door. "Na then, lass," he continued, "these houses were painted at the same time. How is it that she has all this paint left an' thou's noan on?"

This was a region for "open vowels and sharply chiselled consonants" (J.B. Priestley). "Getting on" became an obsession. Mill-town folk even set out to enjoy themselves vigorously, in a more outward fashion than, say, a group from Leeds. A youth-hosteller who met both types told me: "I got the impression that Leeds people enjoyed themselves with pursed lips; those from Bradford and the Heavy Woollen district let out great yells."

Brass, for money, was a favourite word — and affluence a favourite thought. Brass was not used simply for show. A certain meanness was detectable. An Airedale grocer was so mean "he'd nip a currant i' two." A mill-owner was "that tight, if he'd getten a mouth full o' gumboils he'd not part wi' one." This is most picturesque speech, another West Riding characteristic. It was said of a nosey woman who knew everybody's business, that: "If a fly went past her, she'd see it." The West Riding tendency to shout was explained to me by a former Cleckheaton weaver as a consequence of life in the weaving shed. "You don't know you're shouting," she said, "but when you've got to talk ower t'top of all that noise, you sort o' get used to shouting. You don't seem as if you can give up."

Perhaps, at heart, the old struggle for survival in an unfriendly environment was at the heart of the West Riding character. It explains the pre-occupation with "brass". It hints at why the folks of the industrial areas were not silver-tongued; why they tended to be abrupt. Why, indeed, they were dour. They had to struggle against a grim climate, so that on a warm and sunny day a man would say of the weather: "We'll have to pay for this lot!" An inquiry into the state of a man's health led, inevitably, to the comment: "Ah'm nobbut middlin'".

In fact, there are differences of type, and of dialect, as one moves from place to place. Differences in speech mark out the native of Bradford and, say, a man brought up in Huddersfield, which was relatively isolated. The village of Morton, hidden away in its own little fold in the hills, seemed to develop its own intonation and, in some cases, its own dialect. Generation after generation of children were taught at the village school, and so this dialect — so hard to interpret by "offcomers" — carried through to the mill and on into adult life.

The textile region was — and still is, to some extent, as evidenced by local loyalties — a grouping of hundreds of distinct communities. You could find the Bankfoot-ites at the foot of the bank up to Wibsey. A former resident says that they were quite an independent folk, and showed it in no uncertain manner, from those at the top of the bank in Wibsey itself. Nearby, a similar state of affairs existed between Little Horton, Great Horton and Horton Banktopites. To the chagrin of the "natives" a long steep embankment known as St. Enoch's Road was built from Little Horton on to Wibsey bank almost as if invading their "territory", so as to give the Wibseyites and their electric tram service the most direct route to and from the city. The fact that the adjoining, more gentile, Marshfields suburb had been allowed tacitly to expand in a manner so as to act in part as a buffer between Little Horton and Bankfoot, had also not escaped local wrath.

Almost on the doorstep, southwards, was Odsal Top, where the main road from Bradford split into separate roads proceeding onwards to Wibsey, to Halifax, to Brighouse and Huddersfield and to Cleckheaton, Dewsbury and Mirfield. The Huddersfield road passed straight into Low Moor through which, in part, the Cleckheaton road also proceeded onwards to adjacent Oakenshaw. Low Moor and Oakenshaw people seemed to produce the broadest talk of all, often referred to locally as "Cleckheckmondish". This might have been due to their immediate proximity to the heavy woollen towns. Not unassociated were the Low Moor neighbours verging into Wyke, and yet their speech perhaps had more in common with the continuous run of factory settlements and small towns of the Calder and Hebble area nearby.

Westwards and northwards from Bradford, where the mill and factory presence — other than along the river banks — seemed soon to dwindle out, giving way to the moors and dales, the dialect or the language appeared clearer, less localised, much softer upon the ear. By the 1930s, radio was having its impact. People were travelling further afield so, all in all, the various local dialects quietly gave way to more standard English speech, particularly in business and commercial circles.

## Live Performances

Before the flowering of broadcasting, the music hall had gathered together the strands of local tradition and presented its larger-than-life pictures of people and places. Its hey-day was the late Victorian period. It had begun to decline prior to 1914, and it was virtually gone by the 1920s, being finally a victim of the cinema and the radio.

Vaudeville offered a weekly release for the people from the rigours and austerities of everyday life. Florrie Forde was rapturously received at the Alhambra, Bradford, when she sang "My Girl's a Yorkshire Girl". The Alhambra, opened in 1914, became one of the West Riding's best-known theatres. It staged large shows, with stars of national standing. Here were to be seen celebrities like G.H.Elliott (the chocolate-coloured coon), George Formby (father of the ukelele-playing George) and, of course, Gracie Fields, who had her own sweet ballads of mill town life. For many years Francis Laidler staged annual pantomimes in Bradford, first at the Princes and later at the Alhambra. He achieved special fame through his troupes of young dancers, the Sunbeams. Gladys Stanley, who several times was his leading lady, and became his wife, continued the pantomime tradition after his death.

Before the radio and television encouraged people to remain at home, visiting the theatre was a highpoint of the week. As an example, The Princess Theatre, in Little Horton Lane, was for long in the 1930s the home of repertory. A seat in the "gods" here was an experience to be remembered. Two companies established for lengthy seasons were the Terence Byron and the Arthur Brough Players. The few local amateur societies with the backing and financial support to stage their show reached their zenith at the Alhambra. Alfresco Pavilions in the Bradford area were visited by entertainers of the standing of Leslie Henson, Sydney Howard and Reg Bolton. Being a member of a concert party appealed to the musical. At Bradford, Emily Heaton's Merry Minstrels had over 40 members. Performances were usually in hired halls on Saturday evenings. Annually, the Mechanics' Institute was booked for a week, and the shows attracted large numbers of people, most of whom had some family connection with the artistes. "For a concert, admission charges were low, but the cast was quite talented. 'Family entertainment' was provided."

For a time, roller skating was a craze in West Riding towns. It was introduced, as was much else in what became "showbiz", from the United States. Patrons were not allowed on the rink wearing the skates they used on the street, for these were fitted with cast-iron wheels and skates used indoors had hardwood wheels running on ball bearings. Most of the skating rinks were soon to be converted into cinemas.

## At the Cinema

The first cinema show to be given in the Mechanics' Institute at Keighley included a variety turn. When Russell Street Picture House was opened in the town, a front row seat cost a mere 3d, but the patrons sat on hard forms. Each child received a thin stick of garishly-coloured rock after the show. The purpose-built North Street picture house, opened in 1912, had an orchestra. Youngsters paid a penny for a Saturday morning show featuring such stars as Pearl White. A Bradford man remembers when the city had a large number of picture palaces, all vying for custom. "It was not uncommon for a patron in one of the best seats, for which he had paid sixpence or ninepence, to be supplied with a cup of tea and a cigarette, free of additional charge."

At the early cinema, the film broke frequently and sometimes reels did not arrive in time. A cinema in Hipperholme used the films on the same evening as a cinema in Halifax; the reels were transported to Hipperholme by tram, which was sometimes late in arriving, so the audience had to amuse itself until the film arrived. Silent film shows had the obligatory pianists, some of whom were protected from pea-shooting youngsters by transparent screens. At Huddersfield, in about 1908, "Pringles" came to the Co-operative Hall. "How anxious we were for the heroine tied to the pillar in the burning mill!" it is recalled. "Attendance in the following week was a necessity. I don't suppose it cost more than 2d, although that would make a hole in our meagre spending money."

## Outdoor Pleasures

In summer, the brass bands drew crowds to bandstands in the parks. It cost 3d to occupy a chair and a penny for a programme. Across the town went the strains of such familiar tunes as *Wedding of the Rose* and a selection from *Merrie England.* The big Army bands performing in Lister Park at Bradford before the 1914-18 war made a special impression.

The West Riding had its own renowned "men of brass", including the Brighouse and Rastrick Band, which actually began as part of the temperance movement. Albert Modley referred to this group in a song that began: "I'm t' best bloomin' blower in Briggus Brass Band."

Sunday in the park gave people an opportunity to show off in their best attire. Lister Park once had a Sunday morning parade of notables. For example, John Sowden, a famous artist, is remembered as striding in the park wearing top hat, frock coat and dark trousers, gloves and spats, and sporting an orchid in his buttonhole.

In the gala fields, carnivals were attended by comic bands. On May Day, at Bradford, horses and drays belonging to railway, brewery and mill were on parade, beautifully decorated and polished. The drivers devoted hours to cleaning and burnishing the harness. Another popular interest in summer centred on the show, which might be agricultural or floral. Harrogate put on its Flower Show. Even nearer to the Bradfordians were both the Pudsey and Bingley Shows. For the latter, the tram-loading island in the centre of Foster Square itself took on a gala atmosphere. "Crowds queued patiently for the half-hour ride, and everything which could run was sent." The Great Yorkshire Show moved around annually, and lasted several days. "I remember it came to the Woodhall showground, on the Leeds Road, just past the Bradford boundary, in 1934. We were encouraged to go from school and it proved a mighty interesting day. I had never before seen such large and magnificent Shire horses, even though many fine specimens still worked on local roads."

The sporting life of the West Riding would need a book to itself for an adequate description. One could watch cricket in summer, and football of several codes during the colder months. Bradford Northern was popularly known as the "steam pigs"; their first ground was at Park Avenue, from which they moved to Birch Lane, and later to Odsal. The team's red, amber and black shirts were famous. On match days, early this century, it was nothing to see 30 or 40 trams parked on Park Avenue awaiting the dispersing match crowd.

# Demon Drink

BEFORE THE 1914-18 WAR, public houses were open from 6 a.m. to 11 p.m. during the week, and from noon to 2 p.m., and 7 p.m. to 10 p.m., on Sunday. Wartime legislation restricted the opening hours to something like those in force today. Small breweries, including the Devonshire Arms Brewery at Bradford, were absorbed by the big breweries, such as Whittakers, Wallers and Heys, and they in turn were taken over, which limited the choice of drinks. A Great Horton man recalls that in High Street, before the 1914-18 war, there were 12 public houses and three clubs (Liberal, Conservative and Working Men's) in the course of about a mile, "which was fairly typical of Bradford suburbs."

Up to the 1930s, most inns and taverns were run by tenant landlords. In an especially good public house in Airedale one part consisted of the main bar, tap room, singing room and smoke room. The other part was formed of the vaults, with bar and separate entrance. Gentlemen patronised the former, and poorer folk the latter. The patrons warmed themselves at large coal fires.

Every encouragement was given to the public to drink. Before 1914, a clay pipe was supplied free of charge. (Pipes were delivered to a public house or hotel in a sawdust-filled barrel, being packed around the edges, with a dozen or so long "churchwarden" pipes stuck down the middle). Three types of clay pipe were popular—a plain type, one with a moulded bowl adorned by the outline of a lion's head, or some other regal decoration, and a short, stubby, unadorned type. The smoker thumbed "twist" into the bowl of a pipe, and the room in which he smoked soon had the acrid atmosphere of an engine shed.

Beer was delivered in the cask, on drays, and the casks were lowered into pub cellars by rope and tackle. Ale was then somewhat stronger than it is today, and drunkenness was a state more quickly attained. Some men who were stated to be "on the rant" scarcely left a public house for days, and drank steadily. The topers found ways of entertaining themselves. One man specialised in standing on his hands, with his head in a bucket, in which position he managed to sing popular songs!

Good-quality public houses or hotels were staffed partly by young girls recruited in the mining districts; they were paid from 5s. 6d to

8s. 6d a week, all found, in the period before 1914. The brightest girls were trained as barmaids and worked excessive hours.

Drunken brawls were a feature of the town centres on Saturday nights. In Bradford, the brawlers were restrained by a well-loved Catholic priest who was nicknamed "Father Blessing." He was generally respected in the city.

Public morality, backed by legislation, curbed the drinking excesses. The temperance movement urged everyone to sign the pledge. Lantern shows with an anti-drink theme were presented in scores of Temperance Halls on Sunday evenings. At Whitsuntide, the Sunday Schools of Huddersfield joined in a march organised by the Band of Hope; the schools processed through the town to the park, where entertainment included a firework display. Demon Drink was, for a time, on the defensive, yet some taverns continued to use special temptations, such as billiards rooms. In at least one case, patrons had the use of a bowling green.

Albert Cowling, a characterful publican in Bradford, took time off from his business to harry the local authority about the state of the approach road to his home. He bought advertising space in *The Telegraph and Argus*. One advertisement read: "See Naples and die. See the state of Birch Lane and be ashamed of your own city."

# Matters of the Mind

## Religion

ON SUNDAY, A GREAT HUSH descended on the mill towns. Machinery was inactive, the mill fires dozed, few children went out to play, and families — decked in their best clothes — made for the innumerable places of worship. Early this century, a third of the urban population had some association with the Christian religion. The established church, and the chapels of half a dozen major religious denominations, were represented in each place. They were keenly competitive for the souls of men.

Bradford became a cathedral city in 1920, with the elevation to cathedral status of the old parish church of St. Peter. The established church, with its graduate parsons, had a stake in the mill towns, but many of its churches were relatively new. The major religious force was Nonconformity — a chapel, or t'chappil. Among the sweet singers of Zion were Congregationalists, Baptists, Unitarians and Methodists: mainly Methodists. Early this century, the Methodist Church, unlike other denominations, had few middle-class pretentions. It offered a total, warm-hearted, lively fellowship, and highly vocal services. Its range of social activity — never rowdy, of course — would occupy the dedicated person on every night of the week. Methodism proclaimed its own Three R's — Ruin, Redemption, Regeneration.

The chapel offered a welcome to all, including the halt, the weak-witted and the lame. Salvation was assured. Sermons, thrustful though generally repetitive, were delivered mainly by lay preachers who were well-known locally. High peaks of emotion were attained, one peak being the annual rendering of "The Messiah." In the chapel services, and the social round, a worker briefly achieved equality with his employer. He also had opportunities for personal expression in a world where, too often, he must simply obey.

In the period under review, the great period of chapel-building was over. At first, people had met in each other's homes. The new chapels were small, architecturally unpretentious. The monster buildings that succeeded them bore such names as Hebron, Salem, Bethesda, Ebenezer, Providence, Zion, Mount Tabor. With classical facades, they were out to impress, yet — large, square-set, with deep windows — they often managed to look no better than the mills. In due course they looked, within, like the churches of Anglican allegiance.

Between 1900 and 1935, organised religion was in decline. The chapels could still impress their locality at the annual stocktaking, also known as the Whitsuntide Walk, when banners fluttered, bands played, and half the population of a town was on parade while the other half looked on. A woman who lived at Clayton in the 1930s remembers that time because she was given a new straw bonnet and had the excitement of a ride in the milkman's float behind a horse whose mane and tail were bright with plaited ribbons. At the end of the day, each child received a bag of sweets and a new rubber ball, also vast quantities of currant buns and coffee, served at long trestle tables set out in a handy field. At Keighley, "we each took a mug wrapped in a clean handkerchief. The church and chapel were near together, and woe betide if the scholars met. From the Wesleyans came the cry of 'Church Bulldogs' and immediately it was answered by 'Wesleyan dish-clouts'. Our teachers did their best to keep us apart. The long bun that was eaten after the procession was known at Keighley as 'Currant Jonas.'"

Nonconformists were not afraid of demonstrating their religious feelings in public. In this respect, the Salvation Army showed a courage greater than most. A Yeadon woman who had been "saved" knitted dresses and pullovers in Fair Isle. Emblazoned in purple or red across each pullover were the words "God is Love." A chapel goer was noted for his sobriety: he did not drink, swear or gamble. "We were never allowed to have a pack of cards. Once my brother, who had been playing cricket, brought some cards home. Those cards actually belonged to the chapel. Father threw them straight into the fire. He was so against gambling. Father was a right good-living chap." Considerable local status attached to a family who had "a son in the ministry." Several members of the Thursday night class at Cleckheaton went to Canada to train for the ministry—"it was easier to pass there than it was in England"—and eventually they returned, married girls they had known at the chapel, and "took 'em back wi' 'em."

Whitsuntide was the traditional time for children to be arrayed in new clothes, though the suit, dress or coat was perhaps not brand new to the wearer, having been passed on second-hand, after cleaning and perhaps shortening. The best clothes were worn with care. At Anniversary time, some boys "went into long trousers" and they sat before the congregation in an unfamiliar style of clothing, with heads held stiffly vertical by double collars.

Chapel debts were wiped off annually at bazaars. Considerable competition developed between different chapels. In the early 1900s, a man attending Upper Green Congregational Church at Keighley met a worshipper from Temple Street Methodist Church. Upper Green had won first prize in the local Gala, in which they entered a tableau. "Fancy a little place like Upper Green getting the prize," he was told, and he retorted: "Better to be a small place than a large 'un up to its ears in debt." A steward announcing the sum raised by the collections on a special day might, if the sum was favourable, compare it with the amount taken by collections at the other local chapels.

The Bible was given an unqualified acceptance. A man who disliked arguments about religion was heard to say: "If t'Book's reight, it's reight; if not, then clap it at back o' t'fire." A seafarer, returning to a mill town, told a deeply religious old lady of his experiences. He mentioned flying fish, but she could not believe they existed. So he said that when they were in the Red Sea, the ship's anchor was raised. It had "hooked" a wheel that belonged to Pharoah's chariot. "That I do believe," said the old lady, "for it's in t'Bible."

"The Messiah" was presented a hundred times in a hectic West Riding season leading up to Christmas. The mill-town folk took "The Messiah" to heart because it is clear, forthright, warm-hearted. If you listed the dozen most moving experiences in the mill towns, it would surely include a performance of "The Messiah", preferably at Huddersfield. In the largest chapels, the performance was divided into two parts, afternoon and evening. Smaller places contented themselves by rendering selections from the great work, and confining them to single "sittings." A performance in a mission building — a tin tabernacle — was remarkable. The roof leaked in so many places that buckets were deployed to collect the drips. If "Messiah" Sunday was rainy, then cloths were placed in the buckets to deaden the sound of falling water. This small chapel held a choir, the principals, a small orchestra — and, almost as an afterthought, a congregation!

A woman who sang in chapel performances for some 40 years once performed in three different places in a single day. Her feat was excelled at Hebden Bridge, where — so it is said — a man heard parts of the oratorio four times in a day. He rose early, and played part of the work on gramophone records; he heard a wireless version, and attended a performance at a local chapel. In the evening, though it was snowing, he and two or three friends crossed the hills to hear a performance at Oxenhope! It is related that a trumpeter in one mill town — a man weighing an impressive 17 stones — would slip out of the chapel between his solos and imbibe at the nearest public house.

For chapel folk, the Sabbatical hush was absolute. If you washed clothes on a Sunday, you were courting disaster. Two girls decided to give chapel a miss one Sunday evening. They went for a walk, but had gone only a few hundred yards when they heard a heavy crash of thunder. "I don't think anyone went back to church as quickly as we did," one of them related. "We thought it was a judgement on us." The chapels lost their missionary zeal. They became introverted and there were now many competing attractions on a Sunday.

## Politics

MANY OF THE MILL TOWNS were heavily committed to the Liberal cause, which derived support from mill-owners as well as working class folk. Tories at the beginning of this century tended to be the superior industrialists; they were usually supporters of the Anglican church. Politics were taken most seriously, and one keen Liberal thought nothing of walking from Littletown to Cleckheaton to hear the declaration of a poll, however late was the chosen hour. When Lloyd George visited Huddersfield, he spoke in a packed football ground.

In the West Riding, thoughtful men — a number connected with the chapels — sowed some of the seeds of social democracy through a genuine concern for the less fortunate people of the time. A man reared in Bradford recalls hearing whispers of the Independent Labour Party, the British Socialist Party, of Robert Blatchford and his "Ragged Trousered Philanthropists." Bradford had an early and long association with several of the socialist groups. "The founders," it is recalled, "had the craftsmen's skills and strong independence of outlook; they were conscientious and hard-working, straight as they come, tough, sensible but, above all, fair-minded." From various groups there developed the Labour Party, which began to win votes from the Liberals.

The new unions strove for improved working conditions and greater financial rewards for their members. As far back as 1918, the Dewsbury Trades Council pressed for holidays with pay to enable people to enjoy a respite from work without financial hardship. It simultaneously asked for better houses for the mill-workers. There were grim struggles in the early 1920s, and in 1926 came the General Strike. In small, isolated mills, the loyalty of the working folk to their employers remained. At Morton, even during a bitter textile strike, not a single hour of production was lost. A former manager says: "Only one employee was a member of the union, and a more disinterested unionist it would be hard to find."

The 1920s and 1930s were a period of intense social upheaval. During the General Strike, singing workers from Burnley arrived in Bradford and were invited into some of the houses for meals. One visitor was heard to say: "I don't want the earth — just enough to live on, and feed my wife and family." A Keighley woman who watched the marchers from Jarrow arrive in town remembers that her father met some of the men and conducted them to where a meal had been prepared by sympathisers. "He arrived home with a little ragged boy and told my mother that the lad was called Alec, 'and we're keeping him until his family can manage.'"

Mother and grandmother promptly knitted socks for Alec; who had none. They also knitted jerseys for him. "When he went to school with me on the Monday morning, the teacher cried and gave my mother some money to buy him some shoes. Alec stayed with us for some weeks, and my mother wrote to his family every week with news of him. One day the poor woman, Alec's mother, came and cried when she saw how well he looked, and how well clothed he was. She said to my mother: 'Missus, I thank you, for all you've done, but he'll have to come home and share with his brothers and sisters, or he'll grow away from us.' And home he went."


## Culture

WEST RIDING FOLK HAVE, BY AND LARGE, believed that it is better to wear out rather than rust away; to take part in a variety of activities after working hours rather than to sit at home "moping". Hence the proliferation of organisations that can generally be termed "cultural". These range in scale from ambitious musical perform- ances by the world-famous choral society in Huddersfield Town Hall, and concerts by the Hallé in St. George's Hall at Bradford, to meet- ings in which a mere dozen or so enthusiasts gathered to discuss mut- ual interest. Musically, it is a matter of pride that Delius was born in Bradford. As a boy, he rode a pony across the moors to Ilkley. Every district or town had its light opera society and dramatic society. Before the wave of American musicals absorbed the energies of ama- teur entertainers, trained groups joyfully presented the works of Gilbert and Sullivan.

The Bradford Civic Playhouse, inaugurated in 1929 at the home of J.B. Priestley, staged many of his plays. A Baildon man played in *When We Are Married* on no less than 66 occasions. The Halifax Thespians began in 1927, a few years after the first production at Hebden Bridge Little Theatre. The culmination of the efforts of the many West Riding painters was the Spring Exhibition at Cartwright Hall, Bradford.

Culture for everyman came with the radio in the early 1920s. Many recall the crystal sets with headphones, invariably home-made, and the wireless valve which introduced sets with more powerful reception and loudspeakers. Many of these were home-made, using blueprints and instructions provided by new magazines relating to wireless. A man reared in Bradford remembers when components were obtained from specialist shops. One that was well-known in the city was owned by the Super Radio Company, and it lay just off Bank Street. "It did a hectic business. As well as stocking components the shop supplied 'dry' batteries and charging facilities, when these in turn were replaced by wet cell batteries or accumulators." All-mains sets followed. By this time, the mass production of sets enabled more and more families to have the radio. (The never-never system of def- erred payment was now being accepted by the younger folk).

The coming of the radio heralded the age of truly popular tunes. It projected a British way of life, rather than one that was of a small locality. Mill-town folk were now aware, day by day, of the big world that lay beyond the heathered hills dominating their homes.

# Out and About

FOR MANY YEARS, the horse was master of the dusty road. The West Riding saw its first motor vehicles before the start of this century, and the first taxi-cabs appeared in Bradford in 1908. The gradual infiltration of the motor vehicle led to the disappearance of the horse-drawn "growler", landau and hansom.

Just after the 1914-18 war, the carriage proprietors of Bradford lamented an increase in the price of corn. This made it necessary for them to increase the cost of their work (by 2s a pair, and 1s for a single horse). Toby Oxley, who plied for hire in front of Bradford Town Hall, had a matched team of grey horses and a char-abanc. He organised half-day trips to Ilkley or Otley. A full-day outing enabled him to take parties to Boston Spa or one of the local race meetings, such as that at Wetherby. A small helper of years ago "rode at the rear of the vehicle to prevent other small boys from 'jumping' a free ride. When Toby halted his outfit at a public house, and he and the passengers went inside, I got buckets of water for the horses, stirring into the water a powder, which I believe was to prevent the animals from getting colic. At steep hills like Hollins Hill, the able-bodied men walked, or even gave a helping push."

Families with means could hire horse and cab from a livery stable on a Sunday afternoon and be conveyed to a country pub. A Keighley family who went to Snaygill, Kildwick or some other fairly local place found drinks and ham and egg teas. One place specialised in fatty cakes direct from the oven. At another, three large white enamelled basins stood on the kitchen table. One basin contained farm butter, another beef brawn, and the last held dripping. You helped yourself to the havercake hanging on the creel over the fire, and you chose what you had with it."

## Tramways

The horse-drawn, toast-rack type trams that operated in Bradford are recalled as being ill-suited to windy or snowy days. A tram had a roof but open sides. Steam trams "puffed out cindery smoke, which on windy days got in your eyes." The conductor of a steam tram had

71

a highly-polished brass box into which a customer put the fare, either a halfpenny or a penny. The money was dropped into a slot at the top of the box. No tickets were then being issued.

At Huddersfield, it was decided to convert trams to electric traction in 1899. The local steam trams are still recalled. In 1903, the short-lived Mid-Yorkshire Electric Tramway Company, which was presided over by a wool merchant named Alfred Musgrave, began to run between Bradford and Shipley. The service is remembered for its new type of car and the fact that trolley poles were unduly fat. Shipley folk chanted: "Oh, what a line! It starts at Thackley, where nobody lives, and ends at t'cemetery, where they're all dead!" The company lost its identity in 1904, being taken over by Bradford. Shipley took part in the negotiations.

A Huddersfield man, born in 1898, found employment in the Tramways Department, "where on the first day I was taught a lesson which I have never forgotten. I was counting copper when I licked my fingers. Down on my hand came an ebony ruler. There were threats of what would happen if I repeated the act." Huddersfield sent trams to Brighouse, where they came into close contact with tramways operated by Halifax and Bradford. Early this century you could ride a tram from Halifax to Brighouse for thruppence.

A spare-conductor on the Bradford trams in 1929 was given a uniform and the guarantee of a full duty—with full day's pay—only on a Saturday. He otherwise turned up daily, reported his availability (for which he was paid 1s) and got a full duty in his turn only if one was available or extras were needed. Tramway crews were at the mercy of the elements. The driver almost froze to the controls in bad weather. "A limited sop to the harsh conditions was given only in the form of storm capes, top coats with buttons up to the collar, and 'pork pie' regulation hats with flaps that could be dropped to protect the ears. Crews had to be of hardy breed." Christopher John Spencer, a martinet among tramway managers, added to his laurels when he was later given charge of the London company tramways.

It is recalled of the Bankfoot depot that the area round about held a tram-man's colony. "In it so many lived within reasonable access, that they and their families kept together, even off duty. Their world was certainly a different one from the mill. Skilled men with expertise and experience of trades not then required locally, even in the mill, were grateful to don a uniform in the secondary trade of public transport."

The late 1920s saw a flurry of tramcar modernisation. Cushioned transverse seating replaced the old longtitudinal seating in the bottom saloons. In many cases, the refurbishing of seating was on the same basis in the upper saloons. More powerful motors were fitted. "The factory lads and lasses benefited from the extra comfort and, in fact, Bradford used local products in the form of moquette from

THE HEYDAY OF THE TRAM LAY
IN THE 1930s.

Lister's Mill. It was also to become their standard upholstery, for much of the 1930s, in trolley buses and buses.

Leeds put into service, in 1930, at least 100 modern all-enclosed cars. Huddersfield followed with a smaller number in 1931. Both Halifax and Bradford—on narrower gauges—were prevented from using totally enclosed cars, so the fleet had a somewhat vintage appearance, an unfair impression, for they built some new cars." Bradford began to use the trolley bus to replace worn-out parts of its tramway system, whereas the other municipalities favoured motor buses. Keighley gave up the ghost, and came to a financial and working arrangement for its undertaking to be run by the larger *West Yorkshire* company.

The heyday of the tram lay in the 1930s. By this time the tramways were well-established. A tram was of great value when large numbers of people had been moved from the slums to new housing estates at the edge of town, for the tramway provided a handy and inexpensive form of transport. An 11-year old boy, who was regularly given a penny for his tram fare, saved that penny by running furiously ahead of the tram. He did this regularly for weeks and, in due course, he was able to spend 1s. 3d. on a coveted map of Wharfedale.

## The Open Road

The changeover from trams to motor buses was spread over a period of years. At Dewsbury, electric tramways were constructed and operated from 1901, serving the Heavy Woollen District. The company inaugurated motor bus services as early as 1913, and by 1926 there was a fleet of 69 tramcars and 51 omnibuses.

The motor charabanc had been popular for works outings and week-end trips, though the back seats were the last to be filled with passengers. White dust from the untarred roads covered the occupants until they resembled flour-millers. The "charas" did open up the Dales to the mill-town folk. A Keighley woman, recalling a trip to Grassington, said she visited Gracie Pawson, who kept the post office, and asked her if she would make her family some tea. When questioned about the price, Mrs. Pawson said: "Wod sixpence apiece hurt ye?" On one charabanc trip, the tarpaulin split in two places; a thunderstorm broke, and the occupants were half-drowned.

Mechanical vehicles became commonplace in the 1920s and 1930s. Young men scorched on their motor bikes. A popular make, the two-stroke Scott machine, was made at Shipley. Morgan three-wheel vehicles had noisy externally-held air cooled engines. In the 1930s, Morris, Austin and Ford small cars were selling at around £110-£120, and the super-sophisticated Sunbeam-Talbot, one of the earliest "amalgams", was priced at £295. Jowett Cars, of Bradford, produced squat-fronted small cars that sold well to textile families during the 1920s. The firm had a break-through with the "Black Prince" saloon, which seated four (plus) adults on moquette-trimmed seats. Jowett enterprise had seemed well assured when, in 1930, there was a fire at the works and it had a crippling effect on production. "My sister loved working in the Jowett family atmosphere. She was one of many who had to seek work elsewhere as a consequence of the fire," it is recalled.

Prominent among the motor vehicles that carried wool from the ports to the mills were the immaculate vehicles of William Burrill, of Littleborough. The 1930s saw the advent of the large trunk hauliers, including Nicholas Smith (Skipton), Henry Long and Sons (Manningham), Ryburn United, Bouts-Tillotson, Hansons of Huddersfield and Holdsworth of Halifax.

## By Rail

A concentration of mills attracted a complex rail network; it was in evidence from the 1840s. The *Lancashire and Yorkshire* straddled the textile regions. The *Midland* sent trains into Bradford at Forster Square, and Exchange Station was used by the *L & Y* and the *Great Northern*. A devotee of trains mentions that Tingley Junction was a stirring place to visit; it was situated high up and isolated from other groups of buildings, apart from those at the cross-roads. "You were in a little isolated railway world, looking down the valley to Leeds, on

one side, and on another to Morley Town Hall and the Heavy Woolen District."

Following Grouping in 1923, some of the most glamorous trains to operate in and out of the West Riding were to be seen. The LMSR in 1925 introduced a new train, *The Yorkshireman*, with open vestibuled coaches and a first and third class restaurant service provided from a separate kitchen car; it was placed on the London service, operating by Low Moor and Thornhill. In September of the same year, the LNER retaliated with a new Pullman car train between Bradford, Leeds and London and vice versa. It was extended to serve Halifax in 1928, when it became known as *The West Riding Pullman,* later *The Yorkshire Pullman.* Also in 1918, the LMSR gave the name *Devonian* to its prestige restaurant car service from Bradford and Leeds to Bristol and the West of England. The Yorkshire termini were now enlivened by the smart chocolate and cream through-carriages of the *Great Western Railway* from Torquay and Paignton. In the 1930s, both the LNER and LMSR introduced buffet cars for snacks and light refreshments.

In the 1920s and 1930s, rail excursions provided the more restless mill-town families with monthly return tickets at considerably less than standard fares. Day tickets were issued at what today seem absurdly low prices, some of them being 2s.6d for an evening excursion to the seaside, 5s or 6s for a half day outing and 10s for a full day away from home, in which category came a trip to London, with the return frequently overnight. The railways were competing with each other and also with the motor coach.

In June, 1933, the LNER introduced a Sunday "novelty" train (fare 6s) from Bradford by way of York, Alne, Helmsley and over the moors to Whitby, returning by the coastal line through Robin Hood's Bay and Scarborough. Later that year, an excursion from Bradford reached its farthest point at Redcar. Travel agents and newspapers like *The Telegraph and Argus* organised outings on which the patrons went as far as Skye and the Scottish Highlands in a 24 hour period.

## In the Air

Railway Air Services, Ltd., formed by the Big Four railway companies in the mid-1930s, introduced a flight between London and Scotland that called, in both directions, at the joint Leeds/ Bradford aerodrome at Yeadon. Bradford Transport provided a road connection between there and Forster Square station for aircraft passengers. The few people who used that service were easily accommodated in a small Austin Ten staff car and the facility, which failed to attract much support, was discontinued.

## Country Jaunts

Early this century, mill-town folk discovered the countryside with some of the elation felt by explorers who went to the upper reaches of the Amazon. So near, yet so far off because of previously poor transport, were miles of unspoilt open country. A woman who went from Keighley to camp with the Cinderella Club at Grange-over-Sands in 1913 "learnt not to be frightened of sheep, as the fields were full of them." Her luggage consisted of a paper parcel containing a few clothes.

Among the favourite walks from Airedale was that to Dick Hudson's, at the edge of the moors, where callers sampled ham and egg teas. The moors above Baildon and Ilkley were popular. Young children rode the Shipley Glen tramway as a special treat. On Whit Tuesday, in 1900, nearly 20,000 people visited Hardcastle Crags, near Hebden Bridge. Other areas attractive to those with limited means were Shibdendale (near Halifax) and Sunnydale Pleasure Gardens (Hipperholme). The history of Sunnydale began in the 1880s and ended in 1938. It had a maze, two boating lakes and a dance hall, and was "in its pomp" up to about 1930. A woman who, as a teenager, crossed from Airdale to Ilkley one Easter Monday, carried her food in a carrier bag. Long before Ilkley was reached the bottom of the bag fell out! "When we got to Ilkley, a man with a landau drove us along the Grove and back up Brook Street for about 2d. We bought halfpenny canes, and waved to our friends."

Many townsfolk took to the hills as pedestrians. "Way out across the Bronte country, it was odds on there would be contact with Lancastrians from their cotton mill towns — friendly, likeable people, despite their funny ideas about their cricket." Rambling was in favour, and the Ramblers' Association was now a power in the countryside. The Youth Hostels Association, Co-operative Fellowship and Holiday Fellowship helped to meet a keen demand from urban folk who now wanted to be out and about.

A West Riding sense of fun led to the founding of the Ancient Order of Henpecked Husbands, which met annually in the Calder Valley, and the Greeasy Chin Club of Sowerby Bridge, whose inauguration occurred at the end of the 19th century after a gargantuan feast during which men "hed ettun wol their chins were fair greeasy."

## On Two Wheels

Some mill-town cycling clubs began in Victoria's day; others were formed in the cycling boom following the 1914-18 war. Old-timers regard the mid-1920s to the mid-1930s as the golden age of cycling.

The road surfaces were quite good, but traffic was relatively light, and the cyclist was king of the road!

A cycling club usually organised its activities around a "club run," which might be divided into several sections — one for hard riders, another for families, one section for touring and yet another for "potterers." The runs were graded according to the desires and abilities of those taking part. "One of the points about a club run is that you took in new country and went, for instance, to the northern dales, to the Hambledon or Cleveland Hills, or maybe across to the Wolds. The autumn and winter runs were naturally shorter. Social and novelty events — speed-judging contests, hill climbs and treasure hunts — were organised. The annual Holly Run took place just before Christmas. On the first Sunday after Christmas there would be a Christmas Dinner Run, the destination a country pub."

Of the time trials, one led through Acomb and another — named the Triangle — lay in the Pool-Arthington-Harewood area. Road-racing was illegal. In a time trial, each man raced as an individual against the clock. "The competitors were dressed entirely in black, including long black tights, because in the early days of competitive sport the powers-that-be ruled that a cyclist must be inconspicuous... In the reliability trials, the object was to cover 200 miles in 24 hours, riding through the night."

Keen cyclists who were out and about for the day almost always carried their own food. "In those times, a string of pubs, farmhouses and cafes catered for the cyclist; they gave you a space in which to eat your sandwiches, and they plied you with a mug of tea for fourpence. This was re-filled as often as you wished until the nice brown steaming pot of tea became virtually a mug of hot water. It was at least refreshing!" A custom peculiar to the north, especially in winter, was that of taking a tin of soup. "Some catering houses warmed the soup, and they also loaned you a plate and spoon. When the club captain went round to collect the four-pences for pots of tea, he had to remember that so-and-so had a tin of soup warmed. He would need an extra halfpenny for this service, and another halfpenny for the loan of plate and spoon... A similar custom was to be seen at teatime. Then a cyclist would produce a tin of fruit. You'd ask the owner of the eating place to open the tin and provide a dish and spoon. And, of course, he would make a small charge for the service."

In the 1930s, Strakers of Austwick charged thruppence for a pot of tea and a shilling for a meal that included home-made raspberry jam. Hayhursts, by the Green at Bolton-by-Bowland, was a favourite gathering place for cyclists. Others stopped at the *Angler's* at Kilney and the *Queen's* at Litton. A cyclist must be well-nourished. This was not always the case in the depression years, between the wars. If anyone burned up the available calories, the result was "hunger-knock", leading to "bonk", which reduced a cyclist to prostration.

Mrs. Brown, who kept the post office at Malham, made a rich fruit cake. "We cyclists called it anti-bonk cake."

# By the Seaside

SOME WOOLMEN, TAKING ADVANTAGE of an excellent rail service from Bradford to Morecambe, bought seaside homes. Morecambe had become known as Bradford-by-the-Sea. To ordinary folk, a seaside jaunt represented a considerable financial sacrifice in the days of holidays-without-pay. (It was not until 1938 that legislation was introduced concerning paid holidays).

The annual trip to the seaside, for which every family craved, was a blessed release from the everyday grind in a depressing environment. To a family living in the shadow of the mills, in a murky climate, breathing air that was rarely clear of smuts, there was no transition more joyous than a journey to the seaside, where the tide swept grandly on to open beaches, the tones were light, the gulls cried and private enterprise had given to each resort a romantic glitter.

Before 1914, working class folk had to be content with the odd day trip, as organised by chapel or mill. By the 1930s, a period of good and inexpensive rail services, and with private cars now quite common, those families who were not affected by industrial depression took a week's seaside holiday for granted. In 1935, Blackpool was host to a total of 7m visitors between June and September, and Morecambe had 1m visitors. A fair number of those paying guests was from the West Riding.

The holiday weeks had quaint names: Halifax Wakes, Honley Feast, Bowling Tide (Bradford), Meltham and Ripponden Rush-bearings, and Brighouse Rush, which was presumably named after the rush-bearing of many years before, and not the pace at which people quit the town for the summer break. The catchment area for Brighouse station would include something like 30,000 people. Of this figure, possibly no more than 2,000 or 3,000 went away for a holiday, but they all went on the same day. The station was temporarily swamped. Many holiday trains had no corridors. "Once the door closed, you were on your own until you arrived at Blackpool, hours later."

The exodus was mainly in a westerly direction, but a Cleckheaton family of modest means contrived to go east, to Mablethorpe. "We bought tea at Althams every week. For every 4 oz packet, we received a 2d ticket. We saved the tickets, and by holiday time we had enough money to take us to the East Coast. It was a difficult journey; we had to change trains five times! Just before we left home, mother packed a large tin trunk with bread, cakes, boiled tongue, ham, and other food — all we would need to eat while on holiday. Another trunk held our clothes. By Thursday, the bread in the trunk was going mouldy, but none was wasted. Mother simply cut off the mouldy bits and we ate the rest!"

The trunk used for food was nearly as heavy when the family returned home as it had been when they set off. "We filled it with blackberries and mushrooms." At the seaside lodgings, this family was independent. "All we needed was water. Talk about 'down Cheapside.' We children got tuppence a day spending money. I remember they had some pierrots on the sands. Little seats were put out for children to sit on. As soon as we saw the chap with the collection box, we slid off our seats on to the sand!"

Until well into the 1930s, many working class families catered for themselves. They bought their own food, and had it prepared by the landlady. Every family had its own cupboard space. Children of impoverished families could see what others, from more well-to-do homes, were having. There were angry questions — sometimes tears.

At Bowling Tide, life seemed to drain away from Bradford. A woman raised in the 1920s recalls: "The place was overwhelmingly black, with black stone buildings of a sooty, unrelieved drabness, and a sky that was perpetually blanketed by a pall of yellow smoke — except on the occasion of the annual Bowling Tide holiday, when chimneys ceased to belch forth smoke, and the furnaces were raked out, the boilers were cleaned and, for once, the looms were silent. The city emptied of all but essential workers. The rest were busy cooling their feet in the breakers of Blackpool or Morecambe, or rambling over the moors to Dick Hudson's."

During the holiday week, the railways could not manage, alone, to deal with the migratory holidaymakers. "Their road competitors found considerable relaxation in their otherwise normal licensed rigidity for coastal places. Unlimited duplication was permitted. They used it, hiring everything and anything on wheels, including municipal buses, for the Saturdays of the holidays. They would take one town outwards to their holiday destination and then return with a full load to an adjacent town, where the holiday week was ending. It was an effective way of dealing with the problem, and a joy to behold in operation. The railways were just as busy so, all in all, the mill-town holidays were memorable in more ways than one."